*Discovering Christ in Ruth*

# DISCOVERING CHRIST

## IN

# RUTH

## The Kinsman-Redeemer

## Donald S. Fortner

EVANGELICAL PRESS

EVANGELICAL PRESS
Faverdale North Industrial Estate, Darlington, DL3 0PH, England

Evangelical Press USA
P. O. Box 84, Auburn, MA 01501, USA

e-mail: sales@evangelical-press.org

web: www.evangelical-press.org

First published 1999

**British Library Cataloguing in Publication Data available**

ISBN 0 85234 435 X

Unless otherwise indicated, Scripture quotations in this publication
are from the Holy Bible, New King James Version. Copyright ©
1988 Thomas Nelson, Inc.

Quotations marked AV are from the Authorized/King James Version.

Printed and bound in Great Britain by Creative Print & Design Wales,
Ebbw Vale

To
Shelby
my beloved wife, loving companion, and faithful helpmate,
who has honoured me with her devotion for thirty years

# Contents

# 1.
# Christ our Kinsman-Redeemer

*'And he said, "Who are you?" So she answered, "I am Ruth, your maidservant. Spread the corner of your garment over your maidservant, for you are a redeemer"'* (Ruth 3:9, marginal reading).

We will begin our study in the book of Ruth at chapter 3:9, where Boaz said to Ruth, '"Who are you?" And she answered, "I am Ruth, your maidservant. Spread the corner of your garment over your maidservant; for you are a redeemer.' This book, like all the Old Testament Scriptures, speaks of Christ our Redeemer. The subject of this book is redemption. The whole book is a picture of our redemption by Christ, our Kinsman-Redeemer. The key word, used repeatedly in these four chapters, is 'close relative', or 'kinsman' (AV) (2:1,20; 3:9,12,13; 4:1,3,6,8,14). The kinsman is the one who has the right to redeem.

The law of the kinsman-redeemer was given in Leviticus 25:25: 'If one of your brethren becomes poor, and has sold some of his possession, and if his redeeming relative comes to redeem it, then he may redeem what his brother sold.' That prophetic law was given to be a picture of Christ and was fulfilled by him. Our father Adam sold us into bondage and sin, but Christ, our Kinsman-Redeemer, bought us and brought us into liberty, righteousness and life (Rom. 5:19).

The book of Ruth is a beautiful picture of the work of our Lord Jesus Christ as our Kinsman-Redeemer. It shows us both

our need of a Kinsman-Redeemer and the way we may obtain
the blessings of redemption.

There are some people named in these four chapters who
are the primary characters in the book. Their names are mean-
ingful and important. There was a certain man of Israel called
*Elimelech* of Bethlehem in Judah in the days of the judges.
Elimelech means 'God is King'. Yet, when famine came to
Israel, Elimelech took his wife, Naomi, and their two sons,
Mahlon and Chilion, and went down into Moab, a heathen
country where God was neither known nor worshipped. *Naomi*
means 'sweet and pleasant'. *Mahlon* means 'weakness'.
*Chilion* means 'consumption'. *Orpah* means 'stiff-necked and
declining'. *Ruth* means 'companion'.

Elimelech left Israel in weakness and was consumed in
Moab. He died in Moab and left his wife and two sons (1:3).
His two sons married Moabite women, lived with them for ten
years and then died (1:4). Now, poor and broken-hearted,
Naomi determined to go back to Bethlehem (1:6-7). She told
her daughters-in-law to remain with their own people (1:8-13).
Orpah did just that (1:14-15). She went back to her people
and her gods; but not Ruth. She was 'determined to go with'
Naomi (see 1:16-17). So Naomi and Ruth returned to the land
of Israel and to the people of God at the beginning of the
harvest season (1:22).


## A picture of our ruin by the fall of Adam (1:19-21)

When Naomi came back to Bethlehem, everyone gathered
around her, looked at her with astonishment and said, 'Is this
Naomi?' To that she replied, 'Do not call me Naomi [sweet
and pleasant]; call me Mara [bitter], for the Almighty has dealt
very bitterly with me.' She went out young, happy, beautiful
and full; but she came back old, bitter, worn, weary, poor and
empty. That is a picture of us!

Looking at our fallen human race, we might ask of man as we now see him, 'Is this Adam?' Can these poor, dying, corrupt creatures called men be the sons of Adam, who was created in the image of God? (Rom. 5:12; 3:10-19). Man was created a prince, but now he is a pauper. He who was created a king in the garden is now just a beggar. Man, who was created in pleasantness, has fallen into bitterness. Adam was given fulness, but his sons know only emptiness. In the beginning, the race was blessed, but now Adam's fallen race is cursed.

## A picture of Christ's free love to sinners (2:1-16)

Naomi and Ruth came to Bethlehem at the beginning of the harvest season. They were poor. Their allotted inheritance in Israel was gone. They had no one to support them and take care of them. But it was required by God's law in Israel that the poor people be allowed to follow the reapers through the fields and glean, or pick up what the reapers left behind (Lev. 19:9-10; Deut. 24:19).

Ruth knew that a relative could redeem her (2:1). Boaz was such a relative. He was a mighty man. And he was a man of great wealth. She went out into the fields to glean with the poor, hoping she might find favour in the eyes of a relative (2:2). If it were possible for her to have her inheritance among God's people redeemed, Ruth was not willing to perish in poverty. She went to the place where she was most likely to meet her relative, with the hope that he might be gracious to her. As Ruth went to the harvest-fields, where she had the greatest prospect of meeting the one who could redeem her, so sinners in need of mercy are wise to meet with God's people in the house of worship. There Christ walks with and reveals himself to his chosen (Matt. 18:20; Rev. 2:1).

Boaz spotted Ruth and had compassion on her (2:5). There were many poor widows gleaning in the fields, but Boaz set his eyes upon Ruth, took notice of her and had compassion on her before she even knew who he was. In just the same way, the Lord Jesus Christ took notice of us, loved us and chose us before the world was made. He loved us freely from eternity. Let men talk as they may about 'universal benevolence', God's love for his elect is a special, sovereign, distinguishing love (Isa. 43:3-4).

### A beautiful picture of God's special providence (2:1,9,16,18-20)

As the fields of Bethlehem belonged to Boaz, so this world belongs to the Lord Jesus Christ. It is his by design, by decree and by death (Col. 1:16-17; John 3:35; 17:2; Rom. 14:9). As Ruth 'happened to come to the part of the field belonging to Boaz', so God graciously brings each of his elect to the place where he will be gracious to them. As Boaz commanded his young men not to touch Ruth, so the Lord Jesus Christ has given commandment to all creation, saying, 'Do not touch my anointed ones.' As Boaz commanded his men to 'let grain … from the bundles fall purposely' for Ruth, so our Saviour takes care to provide for his elect, even throughout the days of their rebellion and unbelief (Hosea 2:8). Indeed, his angels were created to be ministering spirits to those whom he has chosen to be heirs of his salvation (Heb. 1:14).

### A picture of true repentance (3:1-11)

According to the law of God given to Israel (Lev. 25:25), if a man sold his inheritance and he had a close relative who was willing and able to do so, the relative could buy back his brother's lost inheritance. Boaz had given Naomi and Ruth a reason to hope that he might be willing to redeem them. In chapter 3 Naomi told Ruth what she must do. She told her to go to the threshing-floor where Boaz, the close relative, would be. She told her to humble herself, lie down at his feet and spend the night there — 'and he will tell you what you should do' (3:1-4). And Ruth did what Naomi told her to do (3:5-6).

Ruth marked the place where Boaz would be and went there. She came in softly and lay down at his feet (3:7). The sinner who needs mercy will always be found at the feet of the Lord (Matt. 8:1-2; 15:21-28; Luke 7:37-38; 10:39). Many are too proud to bow as broken, humbled beggars at the feet of Christ. But this woman risked being scandalized. She risked losing the only thing she had left, her name, that she might obtain Boaz's favour.

Ruth plainly told Boaz what she wanted (3:9). In essence, she said, 'Take me. I am your handmaid. Take me for your wife.' Boaz said, 'I will do for you all that you request.' 'But,' he said, 'there is a relative closer than I. He must be dealt with first.' In just the same way, Christ will be merciful. Christ will save. But he could never save anyone until first he had dealt with the law and justice of God. God must be just, even in — especially in — justifying sinners (Rom. 3:24-26).

That brings us to chapter 4. Here we find the last, great picture of this book.

## A picture of Christ our Kinsman-Redeemer (3:11; 4:1-13)

Boaz went up to the gate of the city where men transacted business and met the man who was nearer of kin to Ruth. He said, 'You have first claim upon Elimelech's field. If you want it, buy it.' So the man said, 'I'll buy it!' Then Boaz said, 'If you buy the field, you must also marry Ruth, his daughter-in-law.' Then the man said to Boaz, 'I cannot do that, lest I ruin my own inheritance. You redeem her.' So Boaz bought the field and married Ruth.

The Lord Jesus Christ is our Kinsman-Redeemer. He is our kinsman by his incarnation (2 Cor. 8:9). He is a great and mighty kinsman, for he is himself God (Col. 2:9). He is a kinsman of great wealth. All things are his. All the fulness of grace and glory is in him. As Boaz loved Ruth, so Christ Jesus loved us without a cause, freely. 'We love him because he first loved us!' He says, 'I have loved you with an everlasting love ... with loving-kindness I have drawn you.' As Boaz promised to redeem Ruth, so the Son of God promised to redeem us in the covenant of grace before the world began (Heb. 7:22). But, as with Ruth, there was one who had first claim upon us. The law of God held us as its captors (Job 9:2; 25:4-6). But the law of God says, 'I cannot redeem the fallen one, lest I ruin my righteousness.' The law has a claim upon us, but not the ability to redeem us. The law is our kinsman to condemn us, but could never be our deliverer (Rom. 3:19-20). So the Lord Jesus willingly paid the price of our redemption, the price demanded by the justice of God. By his life of obedience, he magnified the law and made it honourable, and brought in everlasting righteousness for his people. By his death as an atonement for sin, he fully satisfied the wrath and justice of God as our substitute.

As Boaz took Ruth to be his wife, so the Lord Jesus has taken chosen sinners to be his bride (4:13-15). Thank God, he has not left us without a Redeemer. Christ is the 'restorer of [our] life'. He is the 'nourisher of [our] old age'. Like Boaz, our Lord Jesus will not rest until he has 'concluded the matter'. 'He who calls you is faithful, who also will do it.' 'He who has begun a good work in you will complete it.' He 'is able to keep you from stumbling' — and he will. Christ will, at last, present you who are his holy, blameless and above reproach before the presence of his glory.

O love surpassing knowledge,
O grace so full and free!
I know that Jesus loves me,
And that's enough for me!

O wonderful salvation,
From sin Christ set me free!
I feel the sweet assurance,
And that's enough for me!

O blood of Christ so precious,
Poured out at Calvary,
I feel its cleansing power,
And that's enough for me!

Ruth, the pagan Moabitess, became the wife of Boaz, heiress to all his vast estate and great-grandmother of King David, and was placed in the direct lineage of Christ. So also, all who trust him are married to Christ, heirs of God and joint-heirs with Christ, and are made to be the sons and daughters of God Almighty — all by grace, all through Christ our Kinsman-Redeemer!

# 2.
# A very costly move

*'And a certain man of Bethlehem, Judah, went to dwell in the country of Moab, he and his wife and his two sons'* (Ruth 1:1).

## Ruth 1:1-5

Trust in the LORD with all your heart,
And lean not on your own understanding;
In all your ways acknowledge him,
And he shall direct your paths.
Do not be wise in your own eyes;
Fear the LORD and depart from evil

(Prov. 3:5-7).

If Elimelech of Bethlehem, in the land of Judah, had been blessed with the wisdom that God gave Solomon, the history of his family would not be the sad story recorded in the opening verses of the book of Ruth. I do not think I ever read a sadder family history than the one recorded in these five verses. It is a story of famine, death, bereavement, widowhood and constant sorrow. The cause of all this sorrow can be traced to one thing — Elimelech was wise in his own eyes. Rather than trusting the Lord in the time of famine, he leaned on his own understanding and moved to Moab. That proved to be a very costly move.

The book of Ruth is a very short history of the domestic affairs of one family during the days of the judges. It is the story of affliction and comfort, abasement and conversion, great loss and great redemption. The purpose of the book is twofold.

First, the book of Ruth teaches us *to adore the providence of God*. The minute, as well as the great, the private, as well as the public, affairs of our lives are arranged and determined by God's wise and good providence. We ought always to acknowledge and submit to the dispositions of divine providence (1 Sam. 2:7-8; Ps. 113:7-9).

Secondly, the design of God the Holy Spirit in the book of Ruth is *to lead us to Christ*, of whom the book speaks. As we have already seen, Boaz was a type and picture of Christ our Kinsman-Redeemer. But the book also points us to Christ in other ways.

1. Our Saviour, the Lord Jesus Christ, is a direct descendant of Ruth and Boaz. Part of the genealogy given by Matthew comes directly from this book.

2. The conversion of Ruth is symbolic of the calling of the Gentiles. It was always God's intention to save Gentiles as well as Jews. Our Lord Jesus sprang from Jews and Gentiles and is the Saviour of both, the Saviour of the world. As Matthew Henry wrote, 'In the conversion of Ruth the Moabitess, and the bringing of her into the pedigree of the Messiah, we have a type of the calling of the Gentiles in due time into the fellowship of Christ Jesus our Lord.'

3. The whole scene takes place in Bethlehem, the place where our Redeemer was to be born (Micah 5:2).

In these opening verses of the book, Elimelech stands before us as a beacon to warn us of the danger and the costs of unbelief and disobedience. As I read here about Elimelech and his family, I cannot help thinking about Lot and his family. Both men brought great trouble upon their households by the choices they made.

### The time of this trial (1:1)

'Now it came to pass, in the days when the judges ruled...' This is all the information we are given about the date of this trial. But when we read that 'It came to pass,' we understand that it 'came to pass' because God brought it to pass. There are no accidents in this world; famine as well as feasting, trials as well as triumphs are brought to pass by the hand of God, according to the will of God (Rom. 11:36; Eph. 1:11).

This trial took place during the times of the judges, during one of the brightest times of Israel's history. God was King. He ruled Israel by appointed judges. Our greatest trials usually come when they are least expected. The events recorded in the book of Ruth probably took place during the days of Gideon, when the Midianites 'prevailed' and destroyed 'the produce of the earth' (Judg. 6:1-6). I say that because no other time of famine is mentioned during the time when the judges ruled. Also, it must have been near the beginning of this era, because Boaz, who married Ruth, was the son of Rahab the harlot (Matt. 1:5), who received the spies who came to spy out the land (Josh. 2).

We must not fail to observe the fact that, even in the book of Ruth, our Lord Jesus Christ identifies himself with sinners who were the very dregs of the earth. Two of his great-grand-mothers are here identified as Ruth, a Moabitess, the great-grandchild of Lot's incest, and Rahab the harlot. The arms of grace are stretched out to, and embrace, sinners. Christ is the Friend of sinners! He saves sinners. The Lord Jesus Christ came into the world to save sinners, and even in his family tree he shows his mercy towards the ungodly.

**The trial Elimelech faced** (1:1).

'There was a famine in the land.' There was a famine in the land of Canaan, the land 'flowing with milk and honey', the land which once yielded clusters of grapes so big that they had to be carried on a pole between two men (Num. 13:23). Even in Bethlehem, which signifies 'House of Bread', there was a famine. This was one of the judgements which God had threatened to bring upon Israel if they sinned against him (Lev. 26:19-20). The Lord God still exercises judgement among men and nations for their disobedience to him. The hurricanes, floods, tornadoes, earthquakes, famines and diseases which ravage the earth are not acts of nature, but acts of God. When those judgements of God fall upon a land, the righteous suffer with the wicked. Just as the wicked benefit by living near the righteous when God sends the sunshine and rain for his elect, the righteous suffer with the wicked when God pours out his wrath upon the wicked. In the midst of God's providential judgements our only course of action is obedience and faith. Simple as it may sound, it is true:

> Trust and obey,
> For there's no other way
> To be happy in Jesus,
> But to trust and obey!

**Elimelech and his family** (1:1-2)

This is the story of a man, his wife and his children. There may have been many others like him, but the Lord here gives us a very personal look at this one man and his family. It is a story of grace, but it is a story of grace preceded by disobedience, sorrow, death, bereavement and emptiness. Apparently Elimelech's parents were believers. His name means, 'My God is

King.' His very name should have given him comfort in his time of trouble. That which his name taught him should have sustained him. It implied a personal interest in the living God — '*my* God'. And his name declared the sovereign reign of his God over all things — 'My God is King'. His wife's name, Naomi, means 'amiable, sweet and pleasant'. Indeed, Naomi was such a woman. Elimelech was greatly blessed by the Lord. God gave him an amiable, sweet, pleasant woman to be his wife. The names Elimelech gave to his two sons should have warned him of the danger of taking things into his own hands. As we noted in the previous chapter, Mahlon means 'sickness', or 'weakness', and Chilion means 'consumption'. Perhaps Elimelech gave these boys their names because they were sickly children. But their names attest to the fact that the products of our flesh and the most cherished, most pleasant, things of this world are weak, corrupt, fading and dying.


**Elimelech's decision** (1:1-2)

There was a famine in Bethlehem. Elimelech, looking at his situation, judging everything by worldly reasoning, decided to move his family from Bethlehem to Moab. No doubt he hoped to protect his family's wealth and keep them from the hardships God's people were facing in Bethlehem. Apparently, there was an abundance of food and opportunity in Moab. But Moab was a land of idolaters.

Those who are strangers to God often enjoy much more of this world's goods than those who know, love and worship him. As Jeremiah puts it, 'Moab has been at ease from his youth,' whereas Israel has been 'emptied from vessel to vessel' (Jer. 48:11), not because God loves Moab, but because this is 'the portion of their cup' (Ps. 11:6). None should envy Moab, or covet what Moab has (Ps. 92:7). Who would envy the ox being fattened for the slaughter?

We are told that Elimelech 'went to dwell [AV, sojourn] in the country of Moab'. He did not go intending to reside there permanently, but just to stay there for a time. So he took Naomi, Mahlon and Chilion, and came to Moab. But once they got to Moab, they settled down and 'remained there'!

Elimelech's care to provide for his family is to be commended. Nothing is more detestable than a man who will not provide for his own family (1 Tim. 5:8). Over the years I have seen a good many men who tried to use spiritual things to excuse laziness. It doesn't work. True spirituality makes people industrious. A man who will not work does not know God. So we must commend Elimelech for taking care to provide for his family in time of famine. Still, his decision to move to Moab can never be justified. Solomon wrote,

> In the day of prosperity be joyful,
> But in the day of adversity consider:
> Surely God has appointed the one as well as the other
> (Eccles. 7:14).

The day of adversity will either draw us to our God or drive us to the world. If faith does not cling to Christ, the flesh will drag us from him. Did ever a child of God gain anything by going to Egypt for help? What did Lot gain in Sodom? What did David gain at Ziklag? What did Elimelech gain in Moab?

There was no reason for Elimelech to leave Bethlehem. If by some dire necessity he had been forced to sell his property and had been brought into poverty, God's law required his relatives to come to his aid (Lev. 25:25,35). But this was not his condition. He went out full (1:21). Though there was a famine in the land, it was not so severe that people perished by it. Elimelech's neighbours who stayed in Bethlehem, many of them with much larger families than he had, managed to keep body and soul together.

But Elimelech was not content just to live in Bethlehem; he wanted to live in luxury, even if it meant moving to Moab! Rather than lose his riches, rather than be reduced to depending on God to supply his daily bread, Elimelech was willing to disobey and dishonour his God, lead his family away from God and turn his back on the kingdom of God! Suppose everyone had done what he did. Canaan would soon have been empty!

Rather than dealing with trouble, Elimelech tried to run from it. This man, who claimed to be a child of God, whose very name said, 'My God is King', moved to Moab. He took himself, his wife and his family away from the worship of God. He took his family away from, and forsook, the people of God. He led his wife and his sons into the land of Moab and thus to the gods of Moab!

Elimelech's decision was based entirely upon his own understanding, or perception of things, motivated by a completely earth-bound view of things. There was a famine in the land. Therefore, he gave no consideration to the promise of God, the honour of God, his own soul, or the souls of his family. What a very costly decision he made! How very costly this move to Moab proved to be! Yet in his own mind he was no doubt fully justified.

**The disobedience of Elimelech's sons** (1:4)

Mahlon and Chilion 'took wives of the women of Moab'. The opening line of verse 4 might accurately be paraphrased: 'They transgressed the decree of the word of the Lord in taking strange wives.' What they did was in direct violation of God's law. He expressly forbade mixed marriages between the Israelites and the pagan nations around them, just as he forbids the mixed marriages of believers with unbelievers (Deut. 7:2-3;

2 Cor. 6:14). Yet their father must be blamed. He taught them by example the way of disobedience. Parents who raise their children in the lap of the world should not be surprised to see them married to the world. Those who disregard the Word of God, particularly in this matter of marrying an unbeliever, court disaster. Those believers who choose to marry a man or a woman who has no regard for God marry a life of trouble (Deut. 7:3; 23:3; Ezra 9:1-2; Neh. 13:23-27; 2 Cor. 6:14).

**Naomi's desolation** (1:5).

Naomi was reduced to a very pitiful condition: 'The woman survived her two sons and her husband.' What a pathetic condition she was left in! She was now alone and poor, in a strange land, with no one to care for her, and no one with whom she could join in the worship of God. We ought to learn three things from Elimelech:

1. We cannot outrun death. At our appointed time, we shall die.
2. We must never expect to prosper by disobedience: 'Whoever desires to save his life will lose it.'
3. All earthly pleasure and comforts are temporary.

When Naomi lost her husband, she took comfort in her sons. When she lost her sons, she was left alone. True, eternal pleasure and comfort are found only in Christ our God.

**The gracious, overruling providence of God** (Ps. 76:10)

Elimelech did wrong. His family suffered for it. But God's will was done perfectly. Messiah, the Lord Jesus Christ, must be born out of the union of a Moabite woman and the son of Rahab. And so 'it came to pass'! The famine was sent by God because he chose Ruth. Elimelech was allowed to do the evil he did because God was determined to save Ruth. All this came to pass because God purposed to save his elect by the incarnation of his Son, by the life and death of his Son, who was the son of Boaz and Ruth (Rom. 8:28-32).

# 3.
# Three women

*'Therefore she went out from the place where she was, and her two daughters-in-law with her... Then they lifted up their voices and wept again; and Orpah kissed her mother-in-law, but Ruth clung to her'* (Ruth 1:7,14).

## Ruth 1:6-18

The study of Bible characters is one of the most profitable and instructive aspects of Bible study. I like to examine the lives of people as they are set before us in the Scriptures, because the Word of God always gives us an honest representation of them and because they illustrate for us the varied circumstances and conditions of the believer's life in this world. Seeing the hand of God in the lives of others, it is easier for me to understand the Lord's dealings with me.

Naomi had moved to Moab with her husband, Elimelech, and their two sons, Mahlon and Chilion. They had left Bethlehem in a time of famine. But Elimelech had brought his family down to Moab — a pagan, idolatrous land. It had proved to be a very costly move. Elimelech died in Moab. His widow, Naomi, continued to live there for some time. Her sons both married Moabite women, in direct violation of God's express command (Deut. 7:2-3; 2 Cor. 6:14), and they both died childless. Naomi was left in Moab, a widow with two daughters-in-law — three widows in one household, poor, destitute and alone. That is where we take up their story.

Here three women are set before us by God the Holy Spirit. They are introduced to us in the pages of Holy Scripture for our learning and admonition (Rom. 15:4).

*Naomi* was a woman who believed God and, after a time of great trial, returned to the people of God and the place of blessing.

*Orpah* was very much impressed with Naomi and started with her on the journey back to Bethlehem, but at last returned to her people and her gods. Orpah represents those who profess faith in Christ, but do not persevere in faith.

*Ruth* was chosen by God, the object of special grace. Her decision to return to Bethlehem with Naomi was more than an act of love to Naomi. It was an act of faith in Naomi's God, the Lord God of Israel. Ruth is set before us here as a picture of a true believer. True faith endures trials and temptations and perseveres to the end. True faith cannot be destroyed.

These three women, Naomi, Orpah and Ruth, are examples both of what we should, and what we should not be and do.

## Naomi's decision (1:6-7)

Naomi was a woman of remarkable faith. We do not know much about her husband, or her sons, but Naomi was a believer. She left Bethlehem with her husband and she stayed in Moab after Elimelech died, yet her heart was never in Moab. As Lot's wife looked back to Sodom with regret, so Elimelech's wife looked back to Bethlehem with regret. It appears that, by one means or another, all the time she was in Moab she kept up with the news of what was going on in Bethlehem (1:6).

### A work of providence

The providence of God was at work for Naomi. The Lord God always deals with his children as a wise and loving father

(Heb. 12:5-11). Because he loved Naomi, the Lord would not allow her to stay in Moab. He would not permit her to continue there, away from Bethlehem, away from his people, away from his worship. But to get her back he had to deal with her in a very trying way. First, the Lord took away her husband. Then he took both of her sons. He made Moab bitter to her. Thank God for those painful, bitter thorns that hedge up our way and force us to return to him when we are tempted to forsake him (Hosea 2:6-7).

## A *work of the Word*

The Lord caused this chosen one to hear the good report of his grace towards his people. Naomi 'heard in the country of Moab that the LORD had visited his people by giving them bread' (1:6). When Naomi heard what God had done for his people, she believed the message and arose to return to Bethlehem. 'Faith comes by hearing'! By some means or another God got the good news to Naomi that he had visited his people and given them bread. This is the way God saves sinners. He sends a preacher to proclaim the good news of his rich, free, abundant grace. The Lord has visited and redeemed his people. The Bread of Life has come down from heaven. Whenever God brings deliverance to his chosen ones, he causes them to hear the good news of his accomplishments of grace (Rom. 10:17). He never bypasses the use of means — the means he has ordained for the salvation of his people.

## A *believer's work of faith*

'Therefore she went out from the place...' (1:7). There can never be a reconciliation with God without a separation from the world. Those who eat at the Father's table have to leave the feeding-troughs of the world. You cannot serve God and mammon. A choice must be made. 'Choose for yourselves this day whom you will serve!' Naomi had made her choice, and so must we (2 Cor. 6:17; 1 John 2:15). She was determined to leave Moab and return to Israel. She was willing to leave her nearest and dearest relatives. Naomi was a true believer. She knew from whence she had fallen. She knew what she had lost. She remembered how blessed things had been in Bethlehem, and she was determined to return. She counted no cost too great.

## The professions of Orpah and Ruth (1:7-15)

Orpah and Ruth both 'went on the way to return' with Naomi 'to the land of Judah' (1:7). Naomi was an exceptional woman. Though she was a stranger in Moab, both her daughters-in-law preferred living with her to returning to their parent's homes. Not only that, they were ready enough to leave their families to return with Naomi to Bethlehem.

Even though Orpah and Ruth were pagan idolaters, Naomi was kind to them. Without compromising either the glory of God or the truth of God, she lived peaceably in the same house with them. She honoured God and won their affection by her kindness. We could all learn from Naomi (Rom. 12:18). Kindness is always right!

Naomi urged her daughters-in-law to go back to their own families. She commended their behaviour (1:8). She prayed for them (1:9). Then she kissed them goodbye (1:9). But both Orpah and Ruth professed a determination to adhere to their mother-in-law: 'They said to her, "Surely we will return with you to your people"' (1:10). Their emotions were high. They were all weeping and sobbing. And they made an emotional pact. But it did not last. Decisions based upon sentiment and emotion rather than upon sound judgement do not usually last very long.

Then Naomi persuaded both Orpah and Ruth, with strong reasons, to go back to their own families (1:11-13). Why did she discourage them? What was her purpose? Did she not want to save them from idolatry? Did she not want them to worship God? Without question, Naomi wanted both Orpah and Ruth to accompany her to Bethlehem. But if they returned with her, she wanted them to return, not for her sake, but because they wanted to. Those who take up a profession of faith in Christ in order to satisfy someone else, or in the heat of an emotional experience, prove in time to be useless converts. An old deacon and dear friend who is now with the Lord, Darrell McClung, used to say, 'Anything born in the storm will die in the calm.' If Orpah and Ruth did come with her to Bethlehem, Naomi would have them make a deliberate, informed choice. She was not a good 'soul-winner' by today's standards. She was honest. She said, 'If you go with me, it will cost you' (Matt. 8:19-22; Luke 14:28; 18:18-23).

Orpah was easily persuaded to go back to Moab, to go back to her family and to her gods (1:14-15). Orpah's kiss showed that she had affection for Naomi, but she had greater affection for Moab and for all that Moab offered. Like Orpah, many today see great value in Christ and have an affection for him, but cannot and will not follow him, because they simply cannot find it in their hearts to forsake the world. Many Orpahs, because of adversity and excitement, run well for a season. But after a while, like Demas, because they love the world they go back. Frequently they forsake Christ while still making professions of friendship and love towards him!

The motives of every person who professes to be a believer must be tested. Naomi asked, 'Why will you go with me?' (1:11). No earthly inducements were offered. No worldly gain was to be obtained. Nothing but faith in, gratitude to, and love for the Lord Jesus Christ can induce men and women to follow him through thick and thin.

**Ruth's resolution** (1:15-18)

Though Orpah forsook Naomi, and in forsaking Naomi forsook the Lord God, Ruth could not be persuaded to go back:
'Ruth clung to her' (1:14). Grace had chosen her. Providence
arranged all things necessary for her soul's eternal good. And,
at the appointed time, grace fetched her to the throne of God.
Ruth, with complete resolution, walked through the door of
commitment and closed it behind her. In this, she is a pattern
to all who follow Christ.

As she saw in Naomi what Orpah could not, so believing
sinners see the beauty and glory of our Lord Jesus Christ as he
is revealed in us by the grace and power of his Holy Spirit
through the preaching of the gospel (2 Cor. 4:6). We are made
to see who he is — the God-man our Saviour. We are made to
see what he has done for sinners, that he has both brought in
an everlasting righteousness for us by his obedience and fully
satisfied the law and justice of God for our sins by the sacrifice of himself. And God the Spirit has convinced us of the
fulness and perfection of Christ as our mediator.

John Gill informs us that the Chaldean paraphrase of Ruth's
statement suggests that her commitment was more than a commitment to Naomi. It was a commitment to her God, his worship, his will and his people. As such, it represents the declaration made by believing sinners in the waters of baptism. By
that symbolic ordinance (Rom. 6:4-6), being buried with Christ
in the watery grave, believers assert publicly to God, before
all the world, 'I take the Lord God to be my God. I take his
people to be my people. I am resolved that nothing shall separate me from him.' Thus we have bound our souls to him with
an oath, vowing to walk with Christ our God for ever in newness of life. Like Jephthah of old, we have given our word to
the Lord (Judg. 11:35). We cannot go back. Let each one of
us, like Ruth, be resolutely determined to follow Christ all the
days of our lives.

# 4.
# Good news heard in Moab

*'Then she arose with her daughters-in-law that she might re-*
*turn from the country of Moab, for she had heard in the coun-*
*try of Moab that the LORD had visited his people by giving*
*them bread'* (Ruth 1:6).

## Ruth 1:6-7

The Scriptures tell us plainly that when God is pleased to save
a sinner, he causes that sinner to hear the gospel. Ruth 1:6
gives us an illustration of that fact. There is, by divine arrangement, a blessed necessity for gospel preaching. Sinners are
regenerated, born again, given faith in Christ and converted
by the Word of God through the preaching of the gospel. This
is the doctrine of Holy Scripture. All that is needed to con-
vince us of this is a casual reading of the Word of God itself
(Rom. 10:13-17; 1 Cor. 1:21; Heb. 4:12; James 1:18; 1 Peter
1:23-25).

Let people argue and debate all they want to about this
issue. This fact is plainly revealed in Holy Scriptures. God
does not save his elect apart from the preaching of the gospel,
any more than he saves them without repentance and faith.
God does not save chosen, redeemed sinners by the light of
nature, 'sincere' idolatry, a false, man-centred gospel, free will,
works religion, or even the bare reading of Holy Scripture. If
sinners are saved by the mere reading of the Bible, the best
missionary work in the world would be to hire a plane and

drop pages from the Bible all over the world. It is not the
reading of the Word that saves, but the exposition of the Word
in the preaching of the gospel (1 Peter 1:25). Let any who
question this fact simply read the story of Philip and the eunuch
(Acts 8:30-31).

In his exposition of Romans 10:14-17, Martin Luther was
exactly right in declaring that Paul asserts in that passage that
four things are impossible. It is absolutely impossible for anyone to do any of the following:

1. Call upon Christ until he believes on Christ;
2. Believe on Christ until he hears the gospel of Christ;
3. Hear the gospel of Christ without a preacher;
4. Preach the gospel in the power of the Holy Spirit
until he is sent by God.

Whenever men and women realize the necessity and the
value of the preaching of the gospel three things are certain:

1. They will honour God's servants (Isa. 52:7; Rom.
10:15; 1 Thess. 5:12-13);
2. They will attend the ministry of the Word;
3. They will involve themselves in the preaching of
the gospel. They will bring people to hear the gospel.
They will support the work of the ministry, the preaching of the gospel, at home and around the world. And
they will themselves endeavour to tell out the good news
of redemption accomplished by Christ by personal witnessing, distributing tracts, gospel literature, tapes, etc.

**A picture of hearing the gospel** (1:6)

It was when Naomi heard in Moab that the Lord had visited
his people that she left Moab and returned with Ruth to

Bethlehem. The turning-point in the family of Naomi, which was to change the lives of Naomi and Ruth for ever, was what they heard in the country of Moab that the Lord had done for his people.

What a beautiful picture this is of the gospel, the good news that proclaims to sinners what the Lord God has done for his people by the life, death and resurrection of his Son, the Lord Jesus Christ, as their substitute! Naomi 'had heard in the country of Moab that the LORD had visited his people by giving them bread'. Someone told her what God had done for his people. She believed the report (Isa. 53:1). 'Faith comes by hearing, and hearing by the word of God' (Rom. 10:17). She acted upon her faith. Believing God, Naomi abandoned Moab (2 Cor. 6:17; Rev. 18:4) and returned to Bethlehem. There are seven distinct parallels between the Word which Naomi heard in Moab and the hearing of faith.

## 1. A simple message

The message Naomi heard in Moab was a very simple message: 'The LORD had visited his people.' Like Zacharias' prophecy many years later (Luke 1:78-79), the report Naomi heard was of a divine visitation. That is what happened when Christ came into this world. When God visits his people in mercy, salvation is accomplished. The way of peace was opened up by the death of Christ. The light for them that sit in darkness is the gospel.

The gospel of God's free and sovereign grace in Christ is simplicity itself (2 Cor. 11:3). It reveals the most profound mysteries of the universe as simple statements of undeniable truth. Here is a simple *fact*: we have broken God's law (Rom. 3:19-23). Here is a simple *requirement*: justice demands satisfaction (Ezek. 18:20). Here is a simple *declaration*: Christ has visited and redeemed his people (Gal. 3:13). Here is a simple *command*: 'Believe on the Lord Jesus Christ' (Acts 16:31;

Heb. 11:6; 1 John 3:23). Here is a simple promise: 'You will be saved' (Acts 16:31).

Those who are responsible to preach the gospel must do so with clarity and simplicity (1 Cor. 2:1-5,13). True preachers studiously avoid the words of man's wisdom. The power of the gospel is not in the eloquence of the preacher but in the message we preach: 'that Christ died for our sins according to the Scriptures' (1 Cor. 15:1-3). Here are four words that describe the death of Christ and tell us how the Lord visited his people: sovereignty, substitution, satisfaction and success. The Lord Jesus Christ died at Calvary according to his own sovereign will and purpose, according to the terms agreed upon when he became our surety in the covenant of grace before the world began (John 10:15-18; Heb. 10:1-10).

## 2. A message of life

The message Naomi heard in Moab was a message of life: 'The LORD had visited his people by giving them bread.' Bread was the one thing needed, just as Christ, the Bread of Life, is the one thing needed (Luke 10:42). Bread is a common figure and emblem of life, ever illustrative of our Lord Jesus Christ (John 6:32-33,48).

## 3. A message of grace

Naomi's destitute family heard a message of grace down in Moab. They did not hear that the Lord visited his people by providing a means for them to get bread, by making bread possible, by offering them bread, or by giving them a plan by which to get bread, but 'by giving them bread'! Eternal life and all that pertains to it is the free gift of God's unconditional, unqualified grace in Christ (Rom. 6:23).

Satan is a great deceiver. He knows the deceitfulness of the human heart. And he has stocked the world with numerous religions that appeal to the proud heart of man. All satanic religions have one thing in common. They all make salvation to be, in some way, at some point, to some degree, dependent upon, and ultimately determined by, man. The religion of the Bible is the religion of grace — free, sovereign, irresistible grace (Eph. 2:8-9; 1 Cor. 4:7; 15:10). From election and pre-destination to resurrection and glorification there is no part of salvation that is determined by either the will, works, or worth of man. 'Salvation is of the LORD'! It is, in its totality, the work of God's grace in Christ.

*4. Faith demonstrated by works*

Naomi's faith in the word she heard in Moab was shown by her works (1:6-7). All who truly believe God show their faith by their works (James 2:17). God's children do nothing *in order to be* saved, but do much *because they are* saved (Eph. 2:10). We show our faith by coming to Christ (Heb. 11:6). We show our faith by works of love (James 1:27; 2:14-26). It is not legal austerity that demonstrates true faith in Christ, but mercy, love and grace (Rom. 14:17).

*5. Saving faith is a personal, individual matter*

The history of Naomi's family shows us that faith in Christ and salvation by him is a personal, individual matter. Naomi had faith and Ruth had faith. God graciously gave them that gift which no one can have except by the gift of his grace (Eph. 2:8). Orpah only had a profession of faith. There are multitudes like her. Philip Mauro wrote, 'God is a "God of truth", that is to say, of reality; and he will have reality. A mere profession of Christianity ... may deceive men. But God knoweth the hearts.'[1]

*6. Believers look not at what is seen, but at the unseen*

Those who truly believe the gospel of God are controlled in their lives by things not seen (2 Cor. 4:18 - 5:1; Heb. 11:13-16). Orpah went back to Moab, because she 'called to mind that country'. Her mind was full of Moab. Like Lot's wife (Gen. 19:15-26), she started out, but her heart was still in Moab. Ruth had the same opportunity to go back, but her mind was full of another country. Therefore, she persevered.

*7. The difference between saved and lost is all of grace*

The only difference between Orpah and Ruth, the only difference between saved sinners and lost sinners, is the difference made by the grace of God (1 Cor. 4:7). Ruth was not a better woman than Orpah. Both were kind, affectionate, caring and tender daughters to Naomi (1:8-9). But Orpah was lost and Ruth was saved. A sweet, lovable disposition, a tender, affectionate heart and faithfulness in responsibilities and relationships, though they are commendable traits of character, will never take us to heaven. The one thing needed is faith in Christ. If that one thing is lacking, like the rich young ruler, we are yet without hope before God (John 3:15-18; Mark 10:17-22).

Naomi dealt fairly and truthfully with both Orpah and Ruth. She made no appeals to their flesh. She offered no earthly inducements to get them to go back to Bethlehem with her. She simply told them:

> What she had left — her fall, her departure from the house of bread;
> What God had done — how he had visited his people;
> What was to be found at Bethlehem — bread, life, deliverance and restoration if a relative was willing to take up their cause and redeem their inheritance.

Orpah chose to stay in Moab. She counted the cost and went back. Ruth came to Bethlehem with Naomi, believing the report of good news and grace she heard from the lips of her mother-in-law. Once she met and married Boaz, she found with him a better life than she had ever known before.

# 5.
# Ruth's choice

*'Ruth clung to her'* (Ruth 1:14).

Ruth 1:14-17

Great issues are often determined by choices that appear to be insignificant. The choice or decision of one person often affects many. Indeed, there have been a few people in history who made choices and decisions by which God, in his providence, has directed the history of the world. Caesar's decision to cross the Rubicon changed the history of the world for ever. Columbus' decision to continue his western voyage for just one more day was a decision that has affected us all. But by comparison the decisions of those men were insignificant when weighed against the decision made by Ruth the Moabitess in the plains of Moab over 3,000 years ago. The decision of that Moabite stranger fixed for ever the course of human history in the direction of God's eternal, redemptive purpose!

If we learned nothing else from Ruth's choice, we ought to be made to realize the importance of making even seemingly insignificant decisions with wisdom and care. We must always consider the consequences of our decisions. Do not make hasty, rash, spur-of-the-moment decisions. They are almost always costly and regretted. Elimelech made a decision which resulted in the ruin of his family. Ruth made a decision that was costly to herself, but was right and resulted in the salvation, the everlasting salvation, of untold millions. Yet it was a decision, a choice made in a lonely desert, which no one knew about but Ruth, Orpah, Naomi and God.

Ruth's choice involved the complete commitment of herself to Naomi, her people and her God. It is a beautiful and instructive picture of every believing sinner's consecration to the Lord Jesus Christ:

Then they lifted up their voices and wept again; and Orpah kissed her mother-in-law, but Ruth clung to her.

And she said, 'Look, your sister-in-law has gone back to her people and to her gods; return after your sister-in-law.'

But Ruth said:

'Entreat me not to leave you,
Or to turn back from following after you;
For wherever you go, I will go;
And wherever you lodge, I will lodge;
Your people shall be my people,
And your God, my God.
Where you die, I will die,
And there will I be buried.
The LORD do so to me, and more also,
If anything but death parts you and me'

(1:14-17).

## A commitment to walk in Christ's way

Ruth said to Naomi, 'Wherever you go, I will go.' In the course of our lives we cross many paths. Whenever we find ourselves at the crossroads, we all like to reserve to ourselves the freedom to choose which direction we will take. Ruth had no way of knowing what crossroads she might come to. But here she deliberately and decidedly renounced all freedom of choice in the affairs of her life. She committed herself to a path, not knowing where it might take her, only that it would end in Bethlehem. She committed herself to a course of life that would be entirely determined by someone else.

That is exactly what sinners do when they come to Christ. We commit ourselves to him. Taking his yoke upon ourselves willingly, bowing to his will and his dominion as our Lord, we become his voluntary bond-slaves (Matt. 11:28-30; Exod. 21:1-6). This is what we publicly declared to our Lord, to his people and to all the world in our baptism, isn't it? Buried in the watery grave and rising with Christ to walk in newness of life, we publicly avowed that we would, from that day forward, walk with him in newness of life (Rom. 6:4-6). We have been turned from our way to his way. To walk in his way is to walk by faith in the King's highway (Isa. 35:8). That is the highway of holiness, the low way of humility, the narrow way of faith, the rough way of trial, the old way of truth, the safe way of security and the good way of grace. This is the way of the cross that leads us home. What could be more blessed than to have our path ordered by the Good Shepherd, who goes before his sheep in the way in which he leads them?

## A longing to dwell with Christ

'And wherever you lodge, I will lodge.' Ruth made no stipulations as to where the lodging-place should be, or of what kind. The one desire that filled her breast was to be with Naomi, her beloved mother-in-law. She had many friends; but she dwelt with Naomi (2:23). Even when she married Boaz, Ruth clung to Naomi (4:15; cf. 2:14).

This is a picture of every believer's great ambition and blessed prospect — to dwell with Christ (Ps. 27:4; 23:6; Isa.

57:15; John 14:23). It does not matter where my path takes me, if Christ is there. It does not matter where I live, if Christ is there. It does not matter where I worship, if Christ is there. It does not matter what, or where, heaven is, if Christ is there. This is the blessedness of the New Jerusalem: the Lord is there! (John 14:3; Rev. 21:3).

## A commitment to a new set of relationships

'Your people shall be my people.' Ruth's choice involved a painful separation. She left her people and took Naomi's people as her own. The very first thing God calls for is an affirmation of love by a separation, an alienation of affection, from all natural, earthly relationships. If we are to follow Christ, Christ alone must be considered (Luke 14:25-27). Just as the Lord God passed by Esau, giving him no consideration, to save Jacob (Rom. 9:13), so we must allow no consideration to stand between us and Christ. When God called Abraham, he commanded him to leave his country, his family and his father's house (Gen. 12:1). But Abraham would not let go of his father Terah. So God took the life of Terah (Gen. 11:31-32). Then he brought Abraham into Canaan (Gen. 12:4; Acts 7:1-4). If we desire to follow Christ, there is a very real sense in which we must forsake our own people (Ps. 45:10-11). You can only worship and serve one person. Commitment to Christ not only involves the severance of old relationships; it involves loving, loyal commitment to all his family (see Matt. 12:49-50).

## A commitment to the God of the Bible

Then, Ruth said, 'Your God [shall be] my God.' Without question, this was the most difficult part of Ruth's decision. The natural man clings with the utmost tenacity to his religion and to his gods. It does not matter how degrading the religion is, or how useless the god is; the fact that it is his religion and his god gives it value in his eyes. He resents any reflection upon it. He will fight for his religion. He will die in the defence of his god.

Yet, if we are to follow Christ, we must abandon the gods of our fathers. It is absolutely impossible for anyone to follow Christ without forsaking the religion of Babylon and the gods of Babylon (Rev. 18:4; 2 Cor. 6:14 - 7:1). We cannot worship at the altar of free will and the altar of free grace. We must choose, as Ruth did, between the gods of our fathers and the true and living God, the God revealed in the Bible, the God revealed in the person and work of the Lord Jesus Christ. He who is the true and living God is both sovereign and gracious, just and merciful. He is the God of eternal, electing love, effectual blood atonement and sovereign, irresistible grace.

## A lifelong commitment

Then Ruth said to Naomi, 'Where you die, I will die.' At the very outset, Ruth made her position clear: 'I have made my decision. It is a lifelong commitment. It will not be reversed. Not one step will be retraced. I will be with you to the end!' (see Luke 9:62). This, too, is a picture of faith in Christ.

The believer comes to Christ recognizing that in his death as the sinner's substitute, we died (Gal. 2:19-20; 2 Cor. 5:14; Rom. 6:11). We glory in the cross of Christ, because we died there with him (Gal. 6:14). And the believer's commitment to Christ is a resolute, permanent, persevering commitment (Phil. 3:13-14). With the true believer, faith in and commitment to Christ are not something spasmodic, but a deliberately chosen way of life.

## A hope beyond the grave

'And there will I be buried.' Ruth's life was so interwoven
with Naomi's that she wanted to be buried with her. She could
follow her no further than to the grave. But she followed her
that far. Ruth's allegiance to Naomi *ended* in a common grave,
but the believer's union with and allegiance to Christ *begins* in
a common grave. We are buried with him in baptism (Rom.
6:4; Col. 2:12), yet our burial with Christ looks far beyond the
grave to the resurrection and on to the endless ages of eternity. If we died with him, we shall be raised by him. When we
are raised by him, we shall live together with him for ever:
'And thus we shall always be with the Lord.'

Readers, I hold before you the city of God and this world,
Bethlehem and Moab. I hold before you the Lord Jesus Christ
and this world. I urge you now to follow Christ, to consecrate
yourselves to him in exactly the same way that Ruth consecrated herself to Naomi. I cannot tell you what you may meet
with in the way. But I can tell you that this path is the path of
life and ends in life — eternal life. Let us each make Ruth's
choice our choice: 'Wherever you go, I will go ... and there
will I be buried.'

# 6.
# 'The beginning of barley harvest'

*'So Naomi returned, and Ruth the Moabitess her daughter-in-law with her, who returned from the country of Moab. Now they came to Bethlehem at the beginning of barley harvest'* (Ruth 1:22).

## Ruth 1:19-22

It was no accident that Naomi and Ruth came to Bethlehem 'at the beginning of barley harvest'. They came at this time by the arrangement of God's good providence, and this is here recorded by divine inspiration for our instruction (Rom. 15:4). We read in verse 19: 'Now the two of them went until they came to Bethlehem.' We are not told how long their journey took, or what obstacles they met with along the way, only that they came to Bethlehem, which means 'the House of Bread'. Nothing else is really important. They came to that place where all their needs were met — Bethlehem, the House of Bread! They had come to the right place.

When they came to Bethlehem, they caused a great stir: 'All the city was excited because of them.' Why? Why did the arrival of these two poverty-stricken, travel-weary, ragged and hungry women cause such a stir in Bethlehem? No one would profit by their arrival. In fact, these two women were just two more mouths to feed, bodies to clothe and citizens to protect and provide for from the stores of the city. When I read this verse, I am reminded that there is great excitement in heaven over one sinner who repents (Luke 15:10). There is a scene of great rejoicing in heaven every time a prodigal comes home.

Ruth and Naomi came to the right place. They received a warm welcome. And they came at a good time — 'at the beginning of barley harvest'. The beginning of barley harvest was in late April, in the early springtime. Barley is the first grain that ripens in the spring. It is then that the first-fruits of the earth are brought forth, something on which the Scriptures place such great significance. 'The beginning of barley harvest' was a time of great joy and of great spiritual significance, because it anticipated the redemptive work of Christ, his resurrection glory and the believer's eternal life in him.

## The three annual Jewish feasts

There were three feasts held by the Jews every year. These three feasts were established by the law of God and are full of typical instruction. We read about them in Leviticus 23.

### 1. The Feast of Passover (Lev. 23:4-8)

Actually, this feast originated in Egypt (Exod. 12:1-14). When the judgement of God fell upon the Egyptians, every household in Israel sacrificed a paschal lamb. The blood of the lamb was put upon the door of every house. When judgement fell, God looked on the blood and passed over the house where blood was found. That slain paschal lamb represented Christ our Passover, who was sacrificed for us (1 Cor. 5:7), by whose blood we are saved.

Our Lord Jesus Christ kept the Passover feast with his disciples just before he was crucified as our substitute. It was then that he instituted the Lord's Supper (Matt. 26:17-30).

The Feast of the Passover intimated that the immediate result of Christ's death would be a body of people, a family, a nation, a church, sharing together the benefits of his sacrifice in blessed communion (1 Cor. 10:16).

## 2. *The Feast of First-Fruits* (Lev. 23:9-11)

On the Sunday after the Passover, the Israelites brought a handful of the first-fruits of their harvest and waved it before the Lord. This signified that every product of the soil, every result of man's labour and toil, is of the Lord and belongs to the Lord. It was on this day that our Lord Jesus Christ arose from the grave and became the first-fruits of the resurrection (1 Cor. 15:20-23). All the results of Christ's work on the cross, our redemption and our resurrection, are the works of our great God. And all who were ransomed by the sacrifice of Christ our Passover belong to God as his distinctly redeemed people.

## 3. *The Feast of Pentecost* (Lev. 23:15-21)

This was held seven weeks after the Passover. Pentecost was a time of renewal. The Jews renewed their vows and consecrated themselves anew to the Lord God on the Day of Pentecost. This feast foreshadowed the outpouring of the Holy Spirit upon all flesh after the resurrection and exaltation of our Lord Jesus Christ. It was on this day that the Holy Spirit was given in Acts 2.

## The significance of the Feast of First-Fruits

It is the second of these great, typical feasts (the Feast of First-Fruits) which corresponds to the beginning of barley harvest (see Lev. 23:10-11). Ruth and Naomi came to Bethlehem at the beginning of barley harvest. What spiritual and typical significance is to be seen in this fact?

### *1. It symbolizes the resurrection of Christ*

The Feast of First-Fruits and the beginning of barley harvest definitely foreshadowed the resurrection of our Lord Jesus Christ from the dead (1 Cor. 15:20; Col. 1:18). When we realize that the beginning of barley harvest, the time when Ruth came to Bethlehem, refers to the resurrection of Christ, it takes on a very special meaning. Typically and spiritually, this is an event bursting with gospel truth.

### *2. It illustrates the beginning of new life in Christ*

The beginning of barley harvest, the Feast of First-Fruits, was a time of new life, after the long death of winter. In the wintertime everything dies. The flowers fade, the grass withers, the trees shed their leaves. But in the springtime new life rises out of the earth. So it is in things spiritual.

This present gospel age began with the resurrection of Christ from the grave. Our Lord compares this age to a great field ripe with the harvest (Matt. 13:37-39; Luke 10:2; John 4:35). The field is the world. The seed is the Word of God. The harvest is the end of the world. Just as the beginning of harvest was marked in Palestine by the waving of the first ripe fruit before the Lord, so the beginning of this gospel age was marked by the resurrection of Christ from the dead. This was a time of great joy to our Lord's disciples, and would be to us if we understood its full meaning (Luke 24:50-53). Chosen sinners, redeemed by the blood of Christ, are at God's appointed time born again by virtue of Christ's death and resurrection as their substitute. Every time a sinner is born again he or she becomes a kind of first-fruits unto God (James 1:18). The new birth is the first resurrection which guarantees we shall have part in the second (Rev. 20:6).

### 3. It was held on the first day of the week

This feast was held 'on the day after the Sabbath' (Lev. 23:11). Our Saviour rose from the dead on the first day of the week. Though we have no laws requiring it, and though we do not observe any sabbath day, other than the sabbath of faith, the first day of the week is peculiarly the Lord's Day (Rev. 1:10; Ps. 118:23-24; 1 Cor. 16:2).

### 4. It symbolizes our justification

The Feast of First-fruits was a time of great joy. It symbolized our complete justification by the grace of God through the redemption that is in Christ Jesus. The words 'to be accepted on your behalf' (Lev. 23:11) describe what the resurrection of Christ is to God's elect (Rom. 4:25). His righteousness is 'accepted on your behalf'. His blood is 'accepted on your behalf'. He is 'accepted on your behalf'.

### 5. It was a pledge of more to come

The very word 'first-fruits' means, 'There is more to come.' The sheaf of first-fruits waved before the Lord signified two things. First, it was an acknowledgement that God alone brought the grain out of the earth. Life comes from him. Secondly, it was also a pledge of much more to come. So it is with the resurrection of Christ. It manifests the exceeding greatness of God's power and grace to all who believe (Eph. 1:19-20), and it is the pledge of our own resurrection at God's appointed time (1 Cor. 15:12-13,20-23).

## 6. It was a picture of the gospel age

Though this gospel age has already lasted for nearly two thousand years, it is still 'the beginning of barley harvest'. From the moment of Christ's resurrection, God has, as it were, stopped the clock of time. There are no times and seasons counted in this age. There are no signs to be fulfilled before Christ comes. When you read the Old Testament prophets, they saw no interval between 'the sufferings of Christ and the glories that would follow' (1 Peter 1:11). We are to look upon the coming of our Lord with imminent expectancy. God has stopped the clock, in long-suffering patience, for the salvation of his elect (2 Peter 3:9,15). This is still the beginning of barley harvest.

Philip Mauro wrote, 'The application of this to all who hear and believe the gospel is apparent. The glad message of pardoning love, with the gracious invitation, "Come, for all things are ready," is sent to every part of the world, and is intended even for those who are at the lowest levels of human degradation and need. The words that save (Acts 11:14) can penetrate everywhere; and even those who are cursed by the law, as were the people of Moab, may, through the gospel, become partakers of the unsearchable riches of Christ. For He, by his death, has taken away "the middle wall of partition", the law of commandments in ordinances, which shut Gentiles out from those privileges the law conferred on the people of Israel (Eph. 2:12-16); and now, "by means of the gospel", all that Christ is in the resurrection is shared equally by believing sinners, whether from among the Jews or from among the Gentiles (Eph. 3:6-9). So we may say that every believing sinner comes to Bethlehem, to the House of Bread, to share the "true Bread from heaven", and that he comes at "the beginning of barley harvest", for he comes to *Christ risen from the dead*!'[1]

The gospel we are sent into this world to proclaim is the gospel of the risen Christ. The tendency of most in our day is to make little of the resurrection of Christ, except for the rituals of Easter Sunday. In the New Testament the resurrection of Christ was the burden of apostolic preaching (2 Tim. 2:8). Christ on the cross cannot save you; Christ on the throne does (John 17:2). Christ in the tomb has no saving power; Christ on the throne has. The gospel proclaims Christ alive and reigning! Thank God he died. He died to save his people from the penalty of sin. But he did not stay dead. He lives to save his people from the power and dominion of sin.

### 7. It looks back to the death of Christ

Yet the Christ who is risen from the dead is the very Christ who was crucified for sinners as our substitute. The Feast of First-Fruits and the beginning of barley harvest looked back to the slaying of the paschal lamb, and the resurrection of Christ looks back to the death of Christ, the Lamb of God, and has meaning for us, because he made atonement for us by shedding his precious blood in our place on the cross.

The only other place in the Bible where these words, 'the beginning of barley harvest', are used (2 Sam. 21:9) certainly portrays the death of our Lord Jesus Christ and our glorious redemption by the shedding of his blood.

A brief survey of 2 Samuel 21 gives a very clear picture of the redemptive work of Christ, which was most truly 'the beginning of barley harvest'. The story should be familiar.

Saul had sinned against the Lord by breaking a covenant made in the name of God. He slew the Gibeonites with whom Israel had made a covenant (v. 1). Judgement fell upon Israel because of this sin. God sent three years of famine in Israel. Before God would take away the curse, justice had to be satisfied. The Gibeonites required a just atonement (vv. 4-9).

Atonement could not be made by silver and gold (v. 4; 1 Peter 1:18-20). Atonement could only be made by blood (v. 6). It must be a complete, perfect, entire atonement, represented by the number of men slain (v. 6). Seven is the number of fulness, completion and finality. The atonement could be made by none but men of Saul's house. In the same way, atonement for man's sin could not be made except by the Son of God becoming a man (Heb. 10:1-9). Man sinned and man must die. The atonement was made 'on the hill before the LORD' (2 Sam. 21:9). And the day the atonement was made was 'the beginning of barley harvest'. Though justice demanded a complete sacrifice for sin, mercy spared Mephibosheth the son of Jonathan because of a covenant (v. 7). Once the atonement was made, 'God heeded the prayer for the land,' and the curse was removed (v. 14). Reconciliation was accomplished upon the grounds of justice satisfied.

# 7.
# The resolute consecration
# of true faith

*'Entreat me not to leave you, or to turn back from following after you... Your people shall be my people, and your God, my God'* (Ruth 1:16).

## Ruth 1:16-18

There are two things which need to be made absolutely clear at the outset of this chapter. The first is that good works are not, in any way, a cause or condition of salvation. We are saved by grace alone, through faith alone, in Christ alone (Eph. 2:8-9). The second is that good works are, however, the fruit, consequence and evidence of true, saving faith (Eph. 2:10). No one is born of God who does not bear the fruit of the Spirit (Gal. 5:22-23). If Christ is in a person, that person's life will bear a distinct resemblance to Christ. Anyone who is in Christ is a new creature in him (2 Cor. 5:17).

God the Holy Spirit holds Ruth before us as an example of true faith. This woman's decision to worship and serve the Lord God was followed and evidenced by her determination to go with Naomi to Bethlehem and identify herself with the people of God.

If there is anything plainly taught in Holy Scripture it is this: wherever there is true faith in God, true faith in the Lord Jesus Christ, there is a voluntary, determined consecration of heart and life to him (see Matt. 5-7; Rom. 6; 1 Cor. 6; 2 Cor.

6; Eph. 4; Phil. 2; Col. 3; Heb. 6; James 2; 1 Peter 2; 2 Peter 3; 1 John 3-4).

## Ruth's conversion

Ruth was converted by the grace of God through the godly testimony and influence of her mother-in-law, Naomi. Without question, she was converted by God's grace. All true Christians understand that 'Salvation is of the Lord.' It is God's work alone. Yet our God condescends to use human instruments to accomplish his work. And the instrument God used to save Ruth was Naomi's testimony and faithful witness.

Every child of God ought to long for the privilege of being an instrument in his hands for the saving of his elect. We ought, as instruments in God's hands, zealously to seek the salvation of chosen, redeemed sinners. It is written in the Scriptures: 'He who wins souls is wise' (Prov. 11:30). Like those four men in Luke's Gospel (Luke 5:17-20), let us bring needy souls to the Saviour. We must never use the sovereignty of God and the doctrines of grace as an excuse for indifference to the souls of men or the neglect of our own duties and responsibilities.

Ruth's conversion gave Naomi a reason to rejoice and give thanks to God. Naomi was so melancholy, so dejected that she hardly seems to have taken notice of what the Lord did for Ruth. But she should have rejoiced. True, her afflictions were sharp. She had suffered great losses. Her husband, her sons, her home, her wealth — all were gone. She thought the Lord had dealt bitterly with her. Naomi failed, as we often do, to realize that the Lord always deals graciously with his own, especially when he appears to deal bitterly with them (Rom. 8:28).

Consider what she had gained. True, she had lost everything earthly and material, but she had gained the soul of her daughter-in-law. She should have been rejoicing (Luke 15:10). We are all too much like Naomi! We are often so concerned about ourselves and about the cares of this world that we fail to care for, and minister to, the souls of others, and fail to observe the works and blessings of God's grace.

It appears to have been Naomi's decision to return to Bethlehem which influenced Ruth to trust her God. What a lesson there is here for every believer! One great reason why many have so little influence upon their children, their relatives and their friends is the fact that they do not live in a manner which is consistent with their profession.

G. G. Letters, a preacher who lived a long time ago, said that he was converted at a prayer meeting one Sunday evening. That same night, as his mother sat with her children by the fire, she told them how delighted and thankful she would be if they, as one family, were travelling together on the King's highway. When she said that, young George stood to his feet and said, with a calm, resolute voice, 'I, for one, have decided for Christ.'

Thank God, he does use the influences of the godly to save his people. But it takes more than godly influences to save a sinner. Those godly influences must be accompanied by the power and grace of God the Holy Spirit (John 6:63). Not even the preaching of the gospel can bring forth the fruit of faith in the hearts of men without the life-giving power and grace of the Holy Spirit (1 Thess. 1:5).

Let every father and mother learn from Elimelech and Naomi the importance of obedience and consecration to Christ. Elimelech led his sons away from God to Moab, and they died there. Naomi taught Ruth about God and led her to the Lord God by her renewed devotion. Let us learn from Ruth the necessity of consecration to Christ. Let us, like Ruth, renounce all for God, and 'count all things loss for the excellence of the knowledge of Christ Jesus [our] Lord'.

## Ruth's conflict

Ruth's consecration to the Lord was tested, and ours will be as well. Like Ruth, all who trust Christ, consecrating themselves to the Lord God, will have their faith tested. Their resolution will be tempted. Their consecration will be tried.

One great trial of faith, particularly the faith of young believers, is *observing the sorrows and trials of other believers*. Naomi worshipped God. She was a true believer. Yet she was a poor, penniless, homeless widow. She had lost everything dear to her in this world. It was not an easy trial she had to bear. As we have seen, the Lord took her husband, her sons, her home and all her earthly comforts, that he might have her heart. He would not leave her, and he would not let her leave him (Jer. 32:38-40), but her affliction was a great trial for Ruth's faith to endure.

Ruth's faith was tested in that *she was required to stop and count the cost* of following her Lord (1:11-13). If she was to walk with God, she had to leave Moab; so must we. If she was to live by faith, she had to forsake family and friends; so must we. If she was to be numbered among God's elect, she had to share the lot of God's despised and afflicted people; so must we (Heb. 11:24-26). Like Samuel Rutherford, all who count the cost and follow Christ acknowledge that 'His sackcloth and ashes are better than the fool's laughter!'

Ruth's faith was also tested by *Orpah's apostasy*. Orpah followed Naomi for a while. She made a good start for Bethlehem. However, when she realized what it would cost to be numbered among the people of God, she kissed Naomi and went back to Moab. Like the rich young ruler (Matt. 19:20-22), she decided against God. Like him, she departed reluctantly, but she departed for ever. The Pliables of this world are a grief and disappointment to Christians. Yet, as Bunyan taught us, believers must not be influenced by the falls of men like Pliable.

Ruth's faith was certainly tried by *the humiliation she had to endure* (2:2). She had to glean in the fields of Boaz as a pauper, as a stranger, depending entirely on his charity. In just the same way, you and I must humble ourselves as empty-handed beggars before the throne of Christ.

Her faith was greatly tried, I am sure, by *Naomi's apparent coldness*. 'Ruth clung to' Naomi (1:14), but Naomi was a wise woman. She did not want Ruth to come with her because of pity, but because of conviction. To Ruth, it must have appeared that Naomi did not care for her, but Naomi was more interested in her soul than in her approval. Ruth was not a mere statistic to Naomi, but an immortal soul, bound for eternity.

Ruth's faith must have been greatly tried by *Naomi's sorrow and bitterness*, too (1:20-21). If only Naomi had been able to look into the future, she would have seen that she had greater reason to rejoice now than ever. She was about to be brought into the family from whom the Lord Jesus Christ would be descended! Let us learn to trust God's providence (Rom. 8:28). When our hearts are overcome with sorrow, for the sake of others we might influence we ought to take care that we speak no disheartening word (Ps. 73:15). In spite of all these trials, Ruth 'was determined to go with her', which brings us to our third point.

## Ruth's consecration

She devoted herself to the Lord God of Israel. When she said, 'Your God [shall be] my God,' Ruth declared her allegiance to God. When she said, 'Entreat me not to leave you,' she was declaring her thoughtful resolution and determination in this matter. Like Jephthah, she had given her word to the Lord and could not go back (Judg. 11:35).

The essence of all true faith is a confident consecration of heart and life to the one true and living God, the God revealed in Holy Scripture, the God revealed in the Lord Jesus Christ. Ruth said to Naomi, 'Your God...' — not another god, not Chemosh or Moloch, but Jehovah — 'Your God shall be my God!' Most religious people today have no idea who God is. The imaginary god of their devisings is no God at all. They shudder at the mention of the God of the Bible, whose justice is such that he once destroyed the world in his wrath, burned Sodom and Gomorrah in his fury, drowned Pharaoh and his army in the Red Sea, swallowed up Korah, Dathan, Abiram and their followers into hell and saves sinners only by the blood of his own dear Son!

This God, the one true and living God, the God of mercy and truth, grace and justice, fury and goodness, severity and love, the Lord God of heaven and earth, is the peculiar, distinguishing possession of every believer: 'Your God shall be my God.'

This is every believer's great article of faith: 'I believe in God!' We believe his Word, trust his Son and bow to his rule. God himself is our ruler and law-giver (Ps. 119:35-38). The Lord God is our instructor (Ps. 27:11; 86:11). He is the one in whom we have come to trust (Ruth 2:12). Our faith is in God, that God who is revealed and known in the person and work of our Lord Jesus Christ. We trust him alone for grace, salvation and eternal life.

This is God,
Our God for ever and ever;
He will be our guide
Even to death

(Ps. 48:14).

## Ruth's companions

Being consecrated to God, Ruth was consecrated to his people. She said to Naomi, 'Your people shall be my people.' The fact is, those who love Christ love his people (1 John 3:14). It is impossible to be devoted to Christ without being devoted to his people. When Ruth said, 'Your people shall be my people,' she knew that they were a despised people, but that they were God's people. She knew that they were a people with many faults, but that they were his people. She knew they were a people from whom she was not likely to gain much, but she knew they were God's people. Therefore she chose to be identified with them, and counted it an honour to be numbered among them.

Being a Moabitess, Ruth might well have expected ill-treatment from the Jews. But because Jehovah was their God, Ruth made Naomi's people her people. The only hope of redemption was in Bethlehem. There was no kinsman-redeemer for her anywhere else. Boaz was in Bethlehem. The hope of redemption more than made up for any deficiencies she may have seen in her kinsman-redeemer's people. So it is with the church of God today. Christ's presence with his people more than makes up for their deficiencies.

# 8.
# 'Change and decay
# in all around I see'

*'But she said to them, "Do not call me Naomi; call me Mara, for the Almighty has dealt very bitterly with me. I went out full and the Lord has brought me home again empty. Why do you call me Naomi, since the LORD has testified against me, and the Almighty has afflicted me?"'* (Ruth 1:20-21).

## Ruth 1:19-22

Swift to its close ebbs out life's little day,
Earth's joys grow dim, its glories pass away;
Change and decay in all around I see —
O thou who changest not, abide with me!

I once heard our brother Scott Richardson say, 'Life in this world ain't much. It begins with a slap on the bottom and ends with a shovel full of dirt in your face, and there ain't much in between except bumps and bruises.' Certainly, Naomi would agree with that view.

Naomi was a true believer, once highly esteemed in Bethlehem, a woman of wealth and influence. But during a time of famine, she left her country with her husband and her two sons. When Elimelech and Naomi might have used their riches to relieve great need, they chose to hang on to their money and leave their people. But things changed in a hurry. After ten years' absence, Naomi returned from Moab bereaved and destitute. She had lost her husband and her two sons, her money and her property. She came back to Bethlehem with nothing but the ragged clothes on her back and a daughter-in-law who was as poor and destitute as she was. How quickly things change! When Naomi arrived in Bethlehem, as she walked down the streets, broken, weary, ragged and worn with age and trouble, the whole town was astonished by what they saw. They said to one another, 'Is this Naomi?' The withered rose is so much unlike the blooming flower that the one bears only a faint resemblance to the other, and Naomi was so unlike the woman who had left Bethlehem ten years earlier that her friends could hardly believe it was the same person: 'Is this Naomi?'

The afflicting hand of divine providence makes great changes, sometimes shocking changes, in a short time. When God chastens, he means to correct, and his chastening rod always has its intended effect (Heb. 12:5-11). Naomi correctly attributed all her troubles to the hand of her God. She learned that everything she had experienced was brought to pass by the hand of her heavenly Father and that it had all been for her soul's good.

## A picture of the Fall

Certainly, Naomi stands before us in this text as a picture of the fall of the human race in our father Adam (1:20-21). If we could get some idea of Adam's condition and circumstances in the Garden of Eden, as God made him, we would look in the mirror every morning and say, 'Is this Adam? God made us full, but now we are empty!' (Eccles. 7:29).

God made man in his own image and after his own likeness (Gen. 1:27). In the beginning, Adam was full. He was perfectly righteous. He was incredibly brilliant. He was spiritual, strong and in complete peace and harmony with both God and his creation. Then Adam sinned, and we sinned in him. Oh, how great was the fall of man! (Rom. 5:12).

Because of that terrible fall, we all bear greater resemblance, by nature, to the devil than to God (Matt. 15:19). We are spiritually empty, void of righteousness and full of sin. Man is no longer spiritual but carnal, no longer wise but foolish, no longer strong but weak. Fallen man is without peace, without God and without hope in his natural condition.

The only remedy for this lost, ruined condition is the cross of our Lord Jesus Christ (John 3:14-16). When Naomi had lost everything, she returned to Bethlehem; she returned to her God and his people. In just the same way, sinners who have lost everything in Adam must return to the Lord God by faith in Christ Jesus. When Naomi returned to Bethlehem, she came home to God.

Bethlehem means 'House of Bread'. In the house of God there is always 'bread enough and to spare'. And there is always a warm welcome in the Father's heart for returning prodigals. The word 'Judah' means 'praise'; Bethlehem in Judah was the place of praise. Naomi and Ruth came out of the place of sorrow and suffering, out of the place of death and despair, into the place of praise. The mercy-seat is the place of praise. There God meets with sinners and declares that they are forgiven. That mercy-seat is Christ (Heb. 9; 1 John 2:2). Bethlehem in Judah was the place of God, the place of his presence, his power, his protection, his promise and his provision. That is what Christ is to all who trust him. He is our divine refuge (Prov. 18:10).

**Great changes**

In this text, Naomi also represents the changing circumstances of life in this world. What changes occur in this world! Every

day something new happens that either elevates or depresses
our spirits.

We rejoice in favourable changes. Naomi had been through
some hard times. But things were about to get much better.
Even in this vale of tears there are some joys that must not be
overlooked or taken for granted. What great joy we have when
our children become mature, responsible adults, when God is
pleased to save them, when they bring grandchildren into the
family! When friends prosper, our hearts rejoice with them.
When someone we love recovers from sickness or a family's
troubles seem to be over, we find joy in change. But our text is
not talking about favourable changes.

The changes Naomi had experienced were afflicting, trying
changes, changes which are hard to endure. Though her friends
appear to have been terribly disturbed by Naomi's great losses,
she was composed. She resigned herself to the will of God.
She spoke honestly, but not scornfully, of the Lord's dealings
with her (1:20-21).

Naomi had endured a very sorrowful trial. She went out
full. At least, she thought she was full. After all, she had everything the world could offer. Her husband was wealthy and
highly respected. Her sons were in good health. Her family
enjoyed social rank and prestige. But when she came home,
things were different. She came home empty.

Let us learn and ever remember that the fulness of this world
is soon gone (Eccles. 1:2-3; 1 Sam. 2:3-5). There is a fulness
that can never be taken away in Christ (Luke 10:42). To be in
Christ, to have Christ, is to be rich in our souls, rich towards
God, rich for ever.

Painful as her troubles were, and though they must be
blamed upon disobedience and unbelief as their cause, Naomi
properly acknowledged the hand of God in them all. She said,
'The Lord has testified against me, and the Almighty has afflicted me.' 'The Lord has brought me home again empty!'
(1:21; cf. 1 Sam. 2:6-8).

The fact is, nothing will give our souls peace and satisfaction in the times of trouble and great sorrow like the acknowledgement of God's hand in our troubles. This is where Job found solace for his soul (Job 1:21). When God took Eli's sons and told him it was because of his sin, Eli comforted his heart in the acknowledgement of God's providence (1 Sam. 3:18). When David's son was killed because of David's sin, he took comfort in the fact that God loved him, in the fact that he is always wise, gracious and just, and he always does what is right and good (2 Sam. 12:20-24). When Shimei publicly shouted abuse at David before his servants, the man after God's own heart took refuge in the purpose, providence and promise of God (2 Sam. 16:9-12). The one by whose hand Naomi had been afflicted and by whose hand she had been brought home was 'the Lord', 'the Almighty' — El-Shaddai. God all-sufficient, God Almighty, the God of covenant faithfulness is the God she had learned to trust and worship (see Gen. 17:1).

Naomi acknowledged the pain she had felt, and still felt, by reason of her long trial. She said, 'The Almighty has dealt very bitterly with me' (1:20). The cup of affliction is a bitter cup. Though it yields the peaceable fruit of righteousness in the end, the experience of it is not joyful, but painful (Heb. 12:11; Job 13:24-26; Lam. 3:15-17). Naomi also acknowledged that the Lord God had dealt with her sharply, because she had given him reason to do so. She said, 'The Lord has testified against me' (1:21). 'He does not afflict willingly' (Lam. 3:33). God had a controversy with her, so he laid the rod to her back that he might retrieve her heart (Job 5:17-18). This afflicted believer, this corrected child, humbly submitted to and acquiesced in the will of God. She said to her friends, 'Do not call me Naomi [Sweetness]; call me Mara [Bitter], for the Almighty has dealt very bitterly with me.'

God will do whatever must be done to correct his erring children and turn their hearts to him again. How many illustrations of this we have in the Scriptures! Naomi is just one.

Naomi lived in Moab for ten years. Lot lived in Sodom a long, long time. Samson did not lose his hair the first time he laid his head in Delilah's lap. David spent a full year without communion with his God. All of them suffered much because of their sinful behaviour. But the Lord God will never lose one of his own. He says, 'Give me your heart,' and if we are his, he will see to it that we do give him our hearts.

### The believer's attitude

What should our attitude be when we see great changes like these in the lives of our friends, or experience them ourselves in God's good providence? May God the Holy Spirit seal to our hearts this portion of his Word by making it beneficial to our souls and by making us useful to one another.

When we see any of God's people suffering great adversity, let us be kind, gracious and sympathetic, even when we know they have brought the trouble upon themselves (Eph. 4:32; Gal. 6:2). Let us relieve them if we are able to, and love them even if we cannot relieve them. When they return, when the Lord has brought them back, we should always receive them into our hearts with open arms. How often? Our Lord says, until seventy times seven. In other words, let there be no limit to our forgiveness of one another, just as there is no limit to our heavenly Father's forgiveness of us.

When the Lord God fills our cup with bitterness, let us seek by his grace to be content, even when we are made to suffer adversity (Phil. 4:12). As Naomi was bettered by her bitter experiences in life and Job was advanced by his adversity (Job 42:10-16), so shall we be at God's appointed time (Rom. 8:28-30). Let us, therefore, set our hearts upon the world to come (2 Cor. 4:17 - 5:1). Though we are unworthy of the least of God's mercies, the Lord God has done great things for us. All things are ours now. Eternal glory and eternal happiness await us. The Lord knows exactly what he is doing.

God moves in a mysterious way
His wonders to perform;
He plants his footsteps in the sea,
And rides upon the storm.

Deep in unfathomable mines
Of never-failing skill
He treasures up his bright designs
And works his sovereign will.

Ye fearful saints, fresh courage take,
The clouds ye so much dread
Are big with mercy, and shall break
In blessings on your head.

Judge not the Lord by feeble sense,
But trust him for his grace;
Behind a frowning providence
He hides a smiling face.

His purposes will ripen fast,
Unfolding every hour;
The bud may have a bitter taste,
But sweet will be the flower.

Blind unbelief is sure to err
And scan his work in vain;
God is his own Interpreter
And he will make it plain.

# 9.
# 'Seek, and you will find'

*'And she happened to come to the part of the field belonging to Boaz, who was of the family of Elimelech'* (Ruth 2:3).

## Ruth 2:1-12

There are three facts revealed in Holy Scripture that need to be written upon our hearts by the finger of God. Our puny brains may not be able to sort out the details. We may not be able to see the consistency of these facts. They may even appear to be contradictory. Yet these three facts are plainly revealed in the Word of God. Faith bows to the Word and receives these things for what they are, the very truth of God.

### Three facts revealed in Scripture

*1. God almighty saves whom he will* (Rom. 9:15-16,18)

He chose some and passed others by. He sent his Son to redeem some, but not others. Christ makes intercession for some, but not others. He sends his Word to some, but not others. The Holy Spirit regenerates and calls some, but not others. All whom the Father chose, the Son redeemed and the Spirit calls will be saved — all of them and no one else, no matter what. 'Salvation is of the Lord'!

Yet our great, sovereign God has ordained the use of certain means, and will not save any sinner apart from the means he has appointed. God will not alter his purpose at all. If Nineveh is to be saved, Jonah, and no one else, must go to Nineveh, because God has determined to save Nineveh through the preaching of Jonah. God knows how to take care of the details. Ask Jonah.

*2. Each of us is responsible for those immortal souls placed by God under our influence* (Ezek. 33:7-9)

Men and women are saved or lost as a direct result of our actions (Ezek. 3:17-19; 1 Tim. 4:16). God's purpose can never be altered or frustrated. What he has purposed he will do. Neither Lucifer nor anyone can overrule him (Isa. 14:24,26-27). Yet, as Satan is responsible for the angels he led to destruction, though not one elect angel fell, so we are responsible for those who are under our influence, though none of God's elect can by any possibility perish.

*3. Every person is responsible for his own soul*

If you seek the Lord, you will find him. He promises that you will (Jer. 29:12-13). If you refuse to seek him, you will perish for ever in hell. If you trust Christ, you will be saved. If you do not believe on the Lord Jesus Christ, you will be damned. Your faith will not add to the number of God's elect; neither will your unbelief alter the purpose of the Almighty (Rom. 3:3-4). If you are saved, it will be because God chose you, redeemed you and called you. If you die in your sins, it will be because you refused to walk in the light God gave you, you refused to hearken to the Word of God, you refused to believe on the Lord Jesus Christ. Your wilful unbelief, not the purpose of God, will be the cause of your everlasting condemnation (John 3:36; Prov. 1:23-33).

In Ruth 2:1-12, Ruth is set before us as a picture of a sinner seeking the Lord. This is the promise of God to sinners: 'Seek, and you will find.' I know that no one will ever seek the Lord who is not first sought out by the Lord. Our seeking him is the proof that we are sought by him. Yet it is everyone's responsibility to seek him. As Ruth sought barley in the fields of Boaz, so needy sinners seek the Bread of Life in the book of God and in the house of God.

## Ruth's only hope was a kinsman-redeemer (2:1)

'There was a relative of Naomi's husband, a man of great wealth, of the family of Elimelech. His name was Boaz.' Everything in the book of Ruth is about the kinsman-redeemer. He is really the centre of attention. The commentaries, for the most part, miss the point of the book. They talk about Ruth. But Ruth talked about this relative who was to redeem her. Her relative Boaz is a type and picture of our Kinsman-Redeemer, the Lord Jesus Christ.

The close relative, according to God's holy law, had the right to redeem (Lev. 25:25). Boaz was Ruth's close relative. He was, as we see in this chapter and those that follow, willing to redeem her, and he was also able to redeem her. He was a man; and the Son of God became a man that he might redeem and save his people (Gal. 4:4-6; Heb. 2:10-18). Boaz was a man of great wealth; and Christ our Saviour has all that is needed to redeem and save his people. He is of great wealth indeed (Col. 2:10). He has perfect righteousness and has made a complete, perfect, blood atonement, and these things are of infinite worth and merit before God. This man's name also points to Christ. Boaz means 'strength'. The Son of God, our Kinsman-Redeemer, not only has all that is necessary to ransom our souls; he has the power to save (John 17:2; Heb. 7:25).

## Ruth was aware of her need (2:2)

> So Ruth the Moabitess said to Naomi, 'Please let me go
> to the field, and glean heads of grain after him in whose
> sight I may find favour.'
> And she said to her, 'Go, my daughter.'

Being humbled by the hand of God, Ruth knew her need of
grace. Before God saves he slays. Before he exalts he abases.
Before he heals he wounds. He never lifts sinners up until he
brings them down. Ruth had resolved that she would be found
among the children of God. She would not go back to Moab.
But if she lived in Bethlehem, she would have to do so as a
poor beggar living upon the grace of another. This she was
willing to do (Ps. 110:3). Grace chose her. Grace created a
need. Grace met her need. That is always God's method of
grace.

## Providence directed her to the field of Boaz (2:3)

> Then she left, and went and gleaned in the field after the
> reapers. And she happened to come to the part of the
> field belonging to Boaz, who was of the family of
> Elimelech.

Divine providence brought Ruth to the place where she
would meet Boaz. Though it made no difference to Ruth in
which field she gleaned, 'She happened to come to the part of
the field belonging to Boaz.'
She had not planned it. In so far as she was concerned, this
was purely accidental. But what 'happened' to her was by the
arrangement of providence. What 'happened' to her determined her marriage to Boaz, her wealth, her everlasting happiness and her position in the genealogy of Christ. What

'happened' to her also brought about the incarnation of her Saviour, the Lord Jesus Christ! The Son of God must come into the world as a descendant of Boaz and Ruth. God purposed it from eternity. Yet Boaz and Ruth would never have married had she not gleaned in his field. This was no accident. What 'happened' to her was God's purpose. Let us ever adore our heavenly Father's wise providence. Let us regard nothing as insignificant. Let us look for and follow the direction of God in the daily affairs of our lives, trusting his will and bowing to it in all things (Prov. 3:5-6).

## Boaz spoke to his servants about Ruth (2:4-7)

> Now behold, Boaz came from Bethlehem, and said to the reapers, 'The LORD be with you!' And they answered him, 'The LORD bless you!'
>
> Then Boaz said to his servant who was in charge of the reapers, 'Whose young woman is this?'
>
> So the servant who was in charge of the reapers answered and said, 'It is the young Moabite woman who came back with Naomi from the country of Moab. And she said, "Please let me glean and gather after the reapers among the sheaves." So she came and has continued from morning until now, though she rested a little in the house.'

Boaz spoke about Ruth and for Ruth in her hearing before he spoke to her. In these verses, the conversation is all about Ruth. It appears to be not so much for Boaz to get information about her as for her to get information about him. We get a hint of this in verse 8, where Boaz says to Ruth, 'You will listen, my daughter, will you not?' implying that all he had said was for her benefit. In the same way, the Lord Jesus often speaks about and for his elect through the preaching of the gospel before he speaks directly to them by the effectual call of his Spirit. Several things here are highly significant.

1. Boaz and his reapers appear to be one (2:4), as our Lord Jesus says he and his servants are one (Matt. 10:40). Those who serve him have his authority.

2. Ruth wisely followed the reapers through the field (2:3). There was no other way for her to get the bread she needed. God's servants are his angels, sent into his field to gather his wheat into his barn (Matt. 13:30). They are his reapers. They search the field of Holy Scripture and gather from the Word of Life bread for his children.

3. Boaz appeared in his field: 'Now behold, Boaz came.' What a blessing for Ruth! When a seeking sinner earnestly follows his reapers through the field of Holy Scripture, the Master is sure to meet him and bless him with that grace which fills his heart and flows through his lips.

4. Boaz and his workers talked to one another about Ruth. The Lord God and his servants talk to one another about his people, too. The reapers talked to Boaz about Ruth. They told him who she was — a Moabitess; where she came from — Moab; and what she had done (2:6-7). That is the way faithful gospel preachers talk to God about the people for whom they labour.

Then Boaz told his servants what to do for Ruth. He told them to do nothing which might harm her, or hinder her (2:9) and to provide for her need (2:16). He commanded them to 'let grain from the bundles fall purposely for her' (2:16). In the same way, the Lord God commands his servants, in preaching the gospel, to give out truths from his Word on purpose for his elect to be able to pick them up and feed on them (Isa. 40:10-11). Gospel preachers are to set before their hearers gospel promises, gospel doctrines, the grace of God and the person and work of Christ (Eph. 1:1-14,15-23; 2:1-10; 3:8). Preaching the gospel is not telling sinners what they must do, or what God wants to do. To preach the gospel is to tell people what God *has done* for sinners in Christ.

### Boaz addressed Ruth directly (2:8-9)

> Then Boaz said to Ruth, 'You will listen, my daughter, will you not? Do not go to glean in another field, nor go from here, but stay close by my young women. Let your eyes be on the field which they reap, and go after them. Have I not commanded the young men not to touch you? And when you are thirsty, go to the vessels and drink from what the young men have drawn.'

Boaz spoke directly to Ruth about what he had said and done. Boaz assured the Moabitess of his gracious intentions, telling her to look to him for everything, telling her simply to trust him. He told her she had come to the right place and not to go anywhere else, and he gave her permission to drink freely of the water drawn by his servants (see Rev. 22:16-17). He assured her of his protection, telling her that none of the men would touch her, rebuke her, reproach her, or shame her (2:9,15-16). He even courted her. Singling her out, Boaz drew Ruth's heart to him and let her know that his heart was towards her (2:14). What a blessed picture this is of the way the Lord Jesus Christ deals with chosen, redeemed sinners, when he sends forth his Spirit at the appointed time of love to call them by his grace and make them willing in the day of his power! (Ps. 65:4; 110:3).

## Ruth's response (2:10)

> So she fell on her face, bowed down to the ground, and
> said to him, 'Why have I found favour in your eyes, that
> you should take notice of me, since I am a foreigner?'

Ruth was astonished and utterly overwhelmed by Boaz's
goodness. His generosity did not make Ruth arrogant or pre-
sumptuous. It had just the opposite effect. It humbled her:
'She fell on her face, bowed down to the ground' (2:10). Ruth
was completely overwhelmed by a sense of Boaz's goodness
and her own unworthiness of that goodness. In the same way,
when a weary, sinful, heavy-laden soul sees the exceeding riches
of God's grace in Christ, he or she bows down to the ground
(Isa. 6:1-5; Acts 9:1-9). It is not the wrath of God that leads
to repentance, but the goodness of God (Rom. 2:4). The ham-
mer of the law breaks up the icy, hard, fallow ground of our
hearts, but it is the grace of God that melts our hearts before
him! (Hosea 10:12; Zech. 12:10).

Bowing in utter humiliation before the goodness of this
great man, Ruth asked, 'Why have I found favour in your eyes,
that you should take notice of me, since I am a foreigner?' She
knew she was a stranger, a Gentile, without any covenant promise, without any rights, without any merit, without anything to
plead before him except her need and his greatness. That is
the way needy sinners respond to the exceeding richness and
fulness of God's grace in Christ. The first response of the renewed heart to the grace of God is to ask, 'Why me?' (2 Sam.
7:18; 9:8). Those who have received grace are always astonished by grace (1 John 3:1). There is only one answer to the
question, 'Why?' Why was I chosen? Why was I redeemed?
Why was I called? God answers plainly: 'I will be gracious to
whom I will be gracious' (Exod. 33:19; Rom. 9:15). He says,
'Yes, I have loved you with an everlasting love; therefore with
loving-kindness I have drawn you' (Jer. 31:3).

## Boaz assured Ruth of his interest in her (2:11-12)

> And Boaz answered and said to her, 'It has been fully
> reported to me, all that you have done for your mother-
> in-law since the death of your husband, and how you
> have left your father and your mother and the land of
> your birth, and have come to a people whom you did
> not know before. The LORD repay your work, and a full
> reward be given you by the LORD God of Israel, under
> whose wings you have come for refuge.'

Ruth was interested in Boaz, sure enough; but that gave
her no comfort. She needed to know if this man was interested in her. It is one thing for me to be interested in Christ,
but is Christ interested in me? That is the matter of real con-
cern. Boaz assured Ruth of two things. In verse 11, he assured
her of his knowledge of and interest in her. In verse 12, he
assured her of God's faithfulness to sinners who trust him.

Notice the wording of that clause in verse 12 describing
Ruth's faith: 'under whose wings you have come for refuge'
(2:12).There is surely an allusion here to the wings of the cherubim overshadowing the mercy-seat. In other words, whether
Boaz intended it to be so or not, the Holy Spirit is here telling
us that faith in God is trusting the one whose blood atonement
was represented in the blood sprinkled on the mercy-seat. It is
there, and only there, in Christ the Lamb of God, that God
meets with sinners in mercy (Exod. 25:22).

'So she gleaned' (2:17). She found bread, mercy, grace and
life. Then she found a husband. Then she received an inheritance — his inheritance. Then she received great honour — his
honour. So it shall be for all who take refuge in Christ, for all
who come to trust under the wings of the Almighty (Heb.
4:16).

# 10.
# The congregation of the Lord

*'Then Boaz said to Ruth, "You will listen, my daughter, will you not? Do not go to glean in another field, nor go from here, but stay close by my young women"'* (Ruth 2:8).

Ruth 2:4-9

In these verses we follow Ruth, the Moabite stranger, from the field of Boaz into his house. There are many instructive lessons to be learned from the reception that was given her. In this chapter, I want to show you some of the privileges and responsibilities of being a part of God's house as they are illustrated by Ruth's coming into the household of Boaz.

## Obedience to God's Word leads to a place in God's house

Ruth found her place in Boaz's house as the result of humble obedience to the Word of God. You will remember that she had humbly taken her place as a gleaner in the fields, because that is what God in his law prescribed as a means for the poor to continue to provide for themselves. Being obedient to the Word of God, she was guided by the hand of divine providence to the field of Boaz and then to the house of Boaz.

That is always the case with God's saints. If a person walks in the light God has given him, God will give him more light.

If you take the Word of God to be a lamp to your feet and a light to your path, if you follow the Book of God, it will guide you in paths of righteousness and lead you to the place of blessedness (Ps. 19:7-11; 119:9).

## Only one name is honoured in God's house

In the house of Boaz the only prominent person was Boaz himself. No prominence, honour, or distinction was given to anyone but Boaz. Even the servant who was 'in charge of the reapers' is left nameless in the Scriptures, because he was really not important. He was only a servant.

So it is in the house of God. Only one person is exalted in the church of God. Only one person is recognized as pre-eminent in the house of God. Only one name is honoured in the household of faith. Honour, recognition and pre-eminence are given to no man but the God-man, the Lord Jesus Christ. We call no man 'holy', or 'reverend', because no man is. That name belongs only to our God (Ps. 111:9). We call no man 'master', or 'doctor', or 'father', because we are all simply brethren (Matt. 23:6-12).

## The responsibility to seek a place in God's house

When a sinner is saved by the grace of God in Christ, he should immediately seek his place in the congregation of the Lord. Sheep are social creatures. The only time you find a sheep alone is when it is sick or wounded. God's sheep are social creatures too. Believers need one another. As soon as a person is saved he or she should, like Saul of Tarsus, join the disciples (Acts 9:26-27). Every saved sinner ought to be committed to one of 'the churches of God', one of 'the churches of the saints' (1 Cor. 11:16; 14:33).

Some things happen to people immediately they are saved. As soon as you are united to Christ by faith, as soon as you trust the Son of God, you are, or you have been immediately:

> forgiven of all sin by his grace (1 John 1:9);
> justified from all things by Christ's righteousness and shed blood (Acts 13:39);
> born again and made a new creature in Christ (1 Peter 1:23; 1 John 5:1);
> given the place of a son or daughter in the house of God (1 John 3:1; Eph. 2:19).

Sinners are born into the family of God, not by natural birth, but by the grace and power of God the Holy Spirit (John 3:5-7). You are born into the church universal, the mystical, spiritual body of Christ. You do not join it.

However, every saved person ought to seek his or her place in a local church, which is the house of God, the congregation of the Lord, the pillar and ground of the truth. Nothing is more important in the life of a believer than the worship of God in his house (Heb. 10:24-25). Nothing is more detrimental to the lives of men and women who bear the name of Christ than the neglect of God's house (Hag. 1:4-6; Zech. 8:9-15).

Two things, and only two things, are required for membership in the house of God. Throughout the New Testament, we see sinners brought into the fellowship of God's church, seeking and being admitted into that fellowship only if they possessed these two things:

> 1. Those who are received as brothers and sisters in the house of God must be believers; they must possess,

by their own profession, the gift of faith in Christ. No-
where in the New Testament were people received into
the fellowship of the saints, or recognized as brethren,
who did not personally profess faith in the Lord Jesus
Christ.

2. Everywhere in the New Testament believer's baptism was also required for admission into the fellowship
of the saints.

I am aware that most people think these are insignificant,
controversial matters, about which we dare not be very dog-
matic. That simply is not that case. These are matters of plain,
clear revelation, about which we must not compromise. It takes
only a casual reading of the book of Acts to see them plainly
set before us (Acts 2:41-47; 8:36-38; 9:18; 10:48; 16:31-33).
All who trust Christ are to confess their faith in him by believer's baptism. And all who come into the house of God pro-
fessing faith in Christ are to be received without 'disputes over
doubtful things' (Rom. 14:1; 15:6-7). The house of God is to
be a place where the Lord's 'new-born babes' may receive the
love, care, protection, guidance, oversight, instruction and
companionship they need.

## The responsibility of the church towards the stranger

The house of God, the church of God, ought to be like the
house of Boaz, an attractive, pleasing haven for weary strangers. When Ruth came to the house of Boaz, she found it to
be a household of generous, kind, gracious people. She was
attracted to the house, not because of its greatness, grandeur
and gold, but because of the grace displayed in the people
who dwelt there. We preach grace — the free gift of God's
best to those who deserve his worst. Let us make certain that

we practise grace. If the grace that we proclaim with our lips is not practised in our lives, it is not likely that we shall see much result from our preaching. Love one another. Forgive one another. Bear one another's burdens. Be kind to one another. Rejoice with one another. Put away envy, jealousy and peevishness. In other words, 'Do not grieve the Holy Spirit of God' (Eph. 4:30). The church of God is not here to entertain sinners on their way to hell; but we are here to serve the souls of eternity-bound sinners for the glory of God. We offer no attractions to the flesh. But we do offer two attractions to weary strangers: a message of grace and a fellowship of grace in the Lord Jesus Christ.

The person who gets the most attention in the house of God should always be the one who needs the most attention. When Boaz came to Bethlehem to greet his reapers and to sit with them in his house, two things stand out.

First, *very gracious salutations* were given by Boaz to his servants, and by the servants to Boaz (2:4). The words, 'The LORD be with you!' and 'The LORD bless you!' contain all that could be desired by us. Boaz (the type of Christ) pronounced all the blessings of grace upon his servants (typical of God's saints in this world). Then, those servants so blessed of God as to be his servants blessed Boaz, wishing him alone to be exalted.

Second, *a very gracious condescension* was made (2:5). Boaz condescended to look upon Ruth and ask, 'Whose young woman is this?' There were many young women working in the fields, but Ruth was the newcomer. Ruth was the stranger. Ruth was the one who needed attention. And she got it. This question was put to 'his servant who was in charge of the reapers'. He represents the pastor, the gospel preacher, whose responsibility it is to know the people to whom he preaches, to know what they need, and to give account of them to God (Heb. 13:17; Jer. 3:15).

**The welcome Ruth received**

Boaz took great care to put Ruth at ease in his house. He seems to have gone out of his way to make her feel welcome, at home and comfortable. Knowing she was a stranger, knowing she probably felt very uncomfortable, he took care to make her comfortable: 'You will listen, my daughter, will you not?' As we have seen, he spoke to his young men about her in her presence, and he spoke directly to her for her comfort. So it is with our Lord (Isa. 40:1-2). In his house, he speaks about chosen sinners in their presence. Then he speaks directly to them by the power and grace of his Spirit, applying the Word effectually to his own, and he does it for the everlasting comfort of their souls.

**The title which Boaz gave to Ruth**

Boaz addressed her as 'my daughter'. This title placed her upon the footing of the highest privilege and greatest blessedness in the household. In the same way, all who come to God by faith in Jesus Christ are the children of God (Rom. 8:16-17; Eph. 1:4-6; Gal. 3:26; 4:6; 1 John 3:1). All the rights and privileges, all the possessions and prospects of the house of God belong as fully to the youngest and weakest member of the family as to the oldest and strongest. This title, 'daughter', also indicates a permanent relationship. When we talk about the family of God, we are talking about a family circle that will never be broken. God will never disown his own. He will not let us leave them. No enemy can ever carry them away, not even one of them!

## What God requires from all his children (2:8-9)

Boaz's first words to Ruth indicate that which our God requires and expects, and deserves, from all his children.

The house of Boaz was something separate and distinct from all the other houses of the land, and he was determined to keep it that way. He told Ruth what her service and occupation was to be. He told her to glean in his fields and drink from his wells: 'Do not go to glean in another field, nor go from here.' He even told her who her companions were to be: 'Stay close by my young women.' It did not matter whether they pleased her. They pleased him. It was her duty to love them, to serve them and to serve Boaz with them. The lessons for us should be obvious: we who are born of God are to separate ourselves from the people of this world, particularly from their ways and their religion, and devote ourselves to the people of God (2 Cor. 6:14-18; 1 John 4:21; 5:1). As she gleaned in his fields, drank from his wells and followed his young women as they worked, Boaz promised Ruth all the protection of his wealth and power in his house (Heb. 3:6).

If we have been given the privilege of a rightful place in the house of our God, let us carefully fulfil our own place in the house. Let us make our companions these people. We must endeavour not to drop our part of the load. Let us seek to serve, not to be served. And let us always take care to give special attention to those who need special attention.

# 11.
# Ruth's reward

*'The Lord repay your work, and a full reward be given you by the Lord God of Israel, under whose wings you have come for refuge'* (Ruth 2:12).

## Ruth 2:12

The book of Ruth is full of instruction to the believing heart. It sets before us the romance of redemption and beautifully portrays the grace of God towards fallen, helpless sinners through the Lord Jesus Christ, our Boaz, our Kinsman-Redeemer. There are several lessons which are continually brought before us as we go through this brief, instructive book of inspired Scripture.

## The danger of worldliness

The book of Ruth opens with a sad, sad picture. Elimelech, a wealthy man, took his money and his family and fled from Bethlehem down to Moab when famine struck the land of Judah. When he died, he left his family, without a trace of good influence, in the idolatrous land of Moab.

Perhaps Elimelech was a believer. We are not told. His parents apparently were, for in the days when there was no king in Israel and every man did that which was right in his own eyes, Elimelech's parents named him Elimelech, which means,

'My God is King.' But Elimelech did not live up to his name. He fled when he should have been faithful. He left the people of God, the Word of God and the worship of God for the sake of temporal, earthly interests (Matt. 13:22; Luke 12:15).

No believer should ever settle in any place where he would not want to leave his family without his influence. I am sure Elimelech had no intention of doing so, but he died in Moab. There he left his family to fend for themselves among pagans, far away from the people of God, the worship of God and the influence of the congregation of the Lord. Some things are more important than financial security. We all need to take to heart what our Lord teaches us about the love of this world (see James 4:4; 1 John 2:15-17).

## The mystery of providence

The book of Ruth illustrates the fact that 'All things are of God' (2 Cor. 5:18). 'For of him and through him and to him are all things, to whom be glory for ever'! (Rom. 11:36). God overruled Elimelech's failure to fetch Ruth out of Moab, because he had chosen Ruth both to be an heir of grace and to be in the genealogy of Christ. When Naomi came back to Bethlehem, she was full of bitterness. Yet within a comparatively short space of time she was called the happiest of women (Ruth 4:14-15).

We read that Ruth 'happened to come to the part of the field belonging to Boaz'. As far as she was concerned, it was altogether accidental. But as one of the many links in the chain of God's purpose, it was ordained and brought to pass by God. What God does in this world he does on purpose (Eph. 1:11; Rom. 8:28). And the purpose of God in all things providential is twofold: first, the glory of Christ (Col. 1:18); and secondly, the saving of his people (Rom. 8:28-29).

## The wonders of redemption

The primary subject of this little book is redemption, redemption by a close relative, a kinsman-redeemer (2:1). As we have seen, Boaz was a picture of Christ in many ways. He was a mighty man (Heb. 7:25), a wealthy man (Eph. 3:8) and a close relative of Naomi and Ruth (Heb. 2:9-18). Two things were required in the law of Moses for the express purpose of foreshadowing our redemption by Christ: first, the next of kin had the right to redeem the inheritance his brother had lost (Lev. 25:25), and, secondly, the relative was to marry the widow of his brother to keep his name and line alive in Israel (Deut. 25:5-10). Boaz did both (Ruth 4:9-10). So did the Lord Jesus Christ as our Kinsman-Redeemer. He who is our Redeemer is also our Husband.

## The super-abounding grace of God

Redemption and grace always go hand in hand. Wherever you find one, you find the other. As with Boaz, those who are redeemed by Christ shall be wedded to Christ. All whom he redeemed, he saves. All whom he redeemed, he forgives. All whom he redeemed, he blesses with all the exceeding riches of his abundant grace. The book of Ruth is a book about grace, the super-abounding grace of God. It shows us a beautiful illustration of God's prevenient grace, by which he prepares the way for his saving grace. Ruth's redemption by and marriage to Boaz portray our Lord's undeserved grace to us. Ruth was a Moabitess, the cursed child of a cursed race. Yet, Boaz loved her, redeemed her and married her. That is a picture of grace, the free, unmerited grace of God to sinners in Christ.

Ruth 2:12 sets before us a picture of the superabundance of God's grace to us. As Boaz invoked upon Ruth 'a full reward' from God for what she had done, so the Lord Jesus Christ invokes upon every believer a full reward from the Lord God.

## A work of faith

The first thing seen in this verse is Ruth's work of faith. Boaz said to her, 'The LORD repay your work, and a full reward be given you by the LORD God of Israel, under whose wings you have come for refuge.'

We understand that faith is a gift of God (Eph. 2:8). Faith is wrought in us by the exceeding greatness of God's almighty power in saving grace (Eph. 1:19). Faith is the work of the operation of God in our hearts (Col. 2:12, AV). If I believe God, it is because of his grace. Yet faith, being produced in us by the power of God the Holy Spirit, is not a passive experience. Faith is a living principle, a grace that works (Gal. 5:6). Faith does something (James 2:14-26). And God will not forget our work of faith and labour of love (1 Thess. 1:3; Heb. 6:10).

As we read the book of Ruth, we should remember that Ruth represents us, sinners saved by grace, God's elect, all who are converted by the power and grace of God. This woman had come to trust God. Naomi had taught both Ruth and Orpah the things of God. No doubt, Orpah believed Naomi's words and was prepared to go with her to Bethlehem, until she realized what it would cost her. When she realized that, she went back to Moab. She believed Naomi, but she did not trust the Lord. But Ruth had come to trust the Lord God of Israel himself. She believed God. She had come to 'take refuge under his wings'.

The metaphor used by Boaz to describe Ruth's faith refers either to the wings of the cherubim overshadowing the mercy-seat, or to the wings of a mother hen. In either case, it speaks of a place of great strength, complete safety, personal care and great comfort. Christ is that hiding-place for sinners. In him, we take refuge under the wings of the Almighty.

Because she believed God, Ruth did what Orpah could not do (2:11). She forsook her own relations. She abandoned all earthly comfort and benefit. She resolved to worship and serve the Lord God of Israel, whom she had learned to trust through Naomi's faithful witness. She had come to trust the covenant-keeping God, of whom her mother-in-law gave faithful witness, who is faithful and true, sovereign and omnipotent, merciful and gracious. Ruth learned to worship and trust the Lord God by Naomi's witness. Naomi told Ruth who God is, what he had done and where he was to be found. And Ruth believed. She believed Naomi's word, but more, she trusted Naomi's God.

**The reward of grace**

As this text speaks of a work of faith, it also speaks of the great reward of God's great grace: 'The LORD repay your work, and a full reward be given you by the LORD God of Israel, under whose wings you have come for refuge.' Here is the super-abundance of God's grace. He rewards our works of faith (faith which he has given) with the full reward of grace (1 Sam. 2:30). This is beautifully demonstrated in Ruth.

She found what she never expected or looked for — a husband. She who was barren bare a son through whom untold millions have been born of God, for her son was the man through whom the human lineage of Christ was directly traced. Like Ruth, we have found in Christ more than a Redeemer and a Saviour. We have found in him a Husband (Eph. 5:25-30).

Being married to Boaz, Ruth obtained an inheritance to which she had no natural claim. Similarly, in Christ, God's elect have obtained an inheritance to which we have no natural claim. Our reward from God is a heritage of grace given to all who believe on the Lord Jesus Christ. The Lord God gives chosen sinners free forgiveness of all sin (Isa. 43:25). He gives every believer the blessedness of a peaceful conscience (Heb. 9:12-14), security 'without fear of evil' (Prov. 1:33), the blessed assurance of all good (Ps. 23; Rom. 8:32), the confidence of merciful, divinely ordered providence (Rom. 8:28), communion with himself and all the fulness of eternal glory (Rom. 8:17). In the last day, our God will grant us the full reward of grace which is the fulness of heavenly glory. 'The LORD will give grace and glory'!

Yes, God will reward his own elect, like all others, according to their works, in strict accordance with absolute justice. He will reward us for the perfect righteousness of Christ. Just as he rewarded our substitute in strict justice for our sins which were imputed to him, so he will reward every believing sinner in strict justice with heavenly glory, because of the perfect righteousness of Christ imputed to us (2 Cor. 5:21; Rev. 20:12-15; 21:27; 22:14).

God's saints will possess all the fulness of heavenly glory, because in Christ they are worthy of it (Col. 1:12; 3:23-24). Are you worthy of heaven? If you are in Christ you are. As Boaz invoked a full reward for Ruth, the Lord Jesus Christ has earned and purchased a full reward for his people, and he gives it to all who trust him (John 17:5,22; Rom. 6:23).

# 12.
# Mealtime with Boaz

*'Now Boaz said to her at mealtime, "Come here, and eat of the bread, and dip your piece of bread in the vinegar." So she sat beside the reapers, and he passed parched grain to her; and she ate and was satisfied, and kept some back'* (Ruth 2:14).

## Ruth 2:14

Ruth was a Moabitess, a stranger in the land of Judah. This Moabite stranger found satisfaction when she was married to Boaz. The courtship that led up to that wedding began in Boaz's barley-field where Boaz invited her to join his reapers at mealtime. As Ruth found in Boaz everything she needed, so every believing sinner finds in Christ, the Bread of Life, everything he needs. In our Saviour's house there is bread enough and to spare.

There is a distinct correlation between the things recorded in the book of Ruth and those that are taught in the book of Ephesians. They are worthy of detailed study.

1. The minute detail of divine providence in accomplishing the purpose of God is evident (Eph. 1:11).

2. Once Ruth was in Bethlehem she went out into the fields to work. All who are brought into the family and kingdom of God are born to serve (Eph. 2:8-10; Titus 2:11-15).

3. The calling of Ruth the Moabitess prefigured the calling of the Gentiles (Eph. 2:11-13,19).

4. The love of Boaz for Ruth was a picture of the love of Christ to us (Eph. 3:18-19; 5:25-27).

5. Boaz's purchase and redemption of Ruth portrayed Christ's redemption and purchase of God's elect (Eph. 5:25; 1:6).

6. As Boaz's love to her was a matter of unceasing wonder to Ruth ('Why have I found favour in your eyes?'), so Christ's love to us, his great grace to us, is an unceasing, wondrous mystery to the believing heart (Eph. 3:8-11,19-21).

7. As Ruth's wedding to Boaz was a lasting, fruitful union, so our union with Christ is an everlasting union and a fruitful one (Eph. 5:30,32; 4:21-25).

As we read the Word of God, we should always look for Christ and pictures of God's rich, abundant grace in him. If we look for pictures of our own souls' experiences, we are sure to find them. Such pictures are everywhere in the book of Ruth. The text now before us suggests several spiritual truths.

**God's people in this world have their mealtimes**

In the Scriptures, the hearing of the Word of God is often compared to a great feast and faith in Christ is compared to eating and drinking (Luke 14:15-24). During the barley harvest, it was common in Boaz's day for men to set up temporary quarters in their fields. There, in the middle of the day, all the workers would be fed and any gleaners who were invited to join them. That is the picture we have before us. Let me use it to show you three things from the Word of God in this regard.

*1. God has given men who are to feed his people*

God's servants who preach the gospel of Christ are God's gifts to his church by whom the souls of men are fed (Jer. 3:15). The one who does the feeding is our Lord himself. His servants simply distribute the loaves and the fishes. They feed the Lord's sheep with knowledge of God, his Word, his ways and his works. And they feed them with understanding. Men who are called and gifted by God to preach the gospel understand the needs of their hearers. Understanding their needs, God's servants feed his people with bread which is suitable for them, the bread of free grace in Christ, the sinners' substitute. They understand that Christ crucified is all the counsel of God (1 Peter 1:23-25).

*2. All who are hungry will be found at the table when the mealtime comes*

It is senseless for preachers to try to force, or coerce, religious people who make an empty profession of faith to come to church when they have no appetite for the things of God. If people are hungry, no one has to beg them to come and eat. Hungry souls gladly eat, no matter who the cook is, no matter what the plate looks like. Give them the bread and water of covenant mercy, the oil and wine of free grace, and God's people will come and eat. Sheep love sheep-food. Goats are more happy with the weeds of works, intellectualism and legality.

*3. God has ordained certain mealtimes for his own*

Many these days despise all order, set times of worship and the discipline of faithfulness. But God has ordained both private and public worship for the feeding of our souls. We neglect these matters at our peril. Particularly, the public ministry of the Word, the preaching of the gospel and ordinances of divine worship have been established by our God for the good of our souls (Eph. 4:8-16; Heb. 10:25; 1 Peter 2:2).

As Mephibosheth was found sitting at the king's table, let us ever be found at the table of divine worship. As the returned prodigal fed upon the fatted calf, let us ever feed upon our crucified Redeemer.

Our God spreads a table before us in this wilderness. It is written: 'You prepare a table before me in the presence of my enemies' (Ps. 23:5). Often we have an unexpected mealtime, during the routine of the day; the Lord visits us with special tokens of grace, dropping sweet morsels into our souls. In the heat of the day, he refreshes our souls. When we are about to face some great trial, though we are unaware of it, he gives us just the food needed to see us through. After heavy, painful, heart-rending trouble, when we are at our most faint, he graciously visits us and feeds us with his Word in such ways as the world can never understand.

## A gracious invitation

The Lord Jesus affectionately invites poor, needy sinners to his banqueting table.

Boaz did not command Ruth to come. He did not order her to come, though he might well have done. Rather, 'Boaz said to her at mealtime, "Come here, and eat."' Those are the tender words of a gracious suitor. Yes, it is true, the Lord Jesus commands all men to repent. He commands all to believe the gospel. And all are responsible to obey his command. Yet he graciously condescends to our low estate. Like a tender suitor who would win our hearts, he invites poor, needy sinners to come to him. I do not debate for a moment the fact that the gospel is a command, but the command of the gospel sounds like a tender, gracious invitation to me (Isa. 1:18-20; Matt. 11:28-30; 22:9; Rev. 22:17).

The poor, needy gleaner in our text was invited by Boaz himself to 'Come'. And the Son of God invites hungry sinners to come to him. Someone suggested that good witnessing is one beggar telling another beggar where he can get a good meal. Ruth was invited to 'eat of the bread'. In the same way, sinners are invited to eat of Christ, the bread of life, and live for ever.

Yet there is more. Boaz invited Ruth to 'dip' her 'piece of bread in the vinegar'. The vinegar here was not vinegar as we know it, but a relish, a sauce, a gravy to give a rich, delicious taste to the bread. So the Lord Jesus bids us dip our piece of bread in the gravy of his grace. Election is the bread; personal election is the gravy. Redemption is the bread; personal redemption is the gravy. Calling is the bread; personal calling is the gravy. Perseverance is the bread; preservation is the gravy. Some like the bread, but not the gravy. Some like the gravy, but not the bread. Believers want both.

Boaz invited Ruth to come to him at mealtime for two obvious reasons: he loved her; and he intended to marry her. So, too, when the Lord Jesus speaks to sinners by his Spirit, it is because of his eternal intentions of love and grace towards them.


**He gives them the bread of life**

As Boaz passed Ruth the parched corn, so our Saviour gives the bread of life to chosen sinners. It takes more than an invitation to save a sinner. It takes more than an offer of grace. It takes an almighty work of irresistible grace (Ps. 65:4; 110:3). While Ruth sat beside the reapers, he passed her the parched corn. How thankful believing sinners are that our God would not take 'No' for an answer from us! He invited; but we were reluctant. He said, 'Come, eat, dip your piece of bread in the gravy,' but we would not obey his voice. So he put the bread of life into our mouths. Like the Good Samaritan portrayed in Luke's Gospel, God our Saviour came to where we were, picked us up and poured in his grace. He shed abroad his love in our hearts. He gave us repentance.

## He satisfies their souls

As Ruth was satisfied at Boaz's table, every believer finds in Christ that which satisfies his soul. Ruth ate all she wanted. She was fully satisfied. When she had finished eating she left much more than she ate, and carried enough home to Naomi to satisfy her as well (2:18). There is bread enough in our Father's house and plenty to spare. Some preachers and some churches seem to think they are to be spiritual protectionists, conservationists of the worst kind. They seem to be afraid that if they share the bread of God's house they will run out of bread. Let us preach the gospel freely to all men, bidding poor, needy, hungry sinners, 'Come and eat!'

# 13.
# Handfuls let fall on purpose

*'And when she rose up to glean, Boaz commanded his young men, saying, "Let her glean even among the sheaves, and do not reproach her. Also let grain from the bundles fall purposely for her; leave it that she may glean, and do not rebuke her"'* (2:15-16).

Ruth 2:15-16

In the Old Testament, under the Mosaic law, gleaning was one of the rights of the people. The farmer was forbidden by God to reap the corners of his fields. If, by some oversight, he mistakenly left a bundle of wheat in his field, he was not allowed to go back and pick it up. It was to be left for the widows, the fatherless and the poor in the land. The same thing was true of their orchards and vineyards.

In the second chapter of Ruth, we see this law of gleaning being fulfilled. The things recorded in this chapter are written for our learning and for our admonition. Indeed, all that is written in the book of Ruth is intended by God the Holy Spirit to show us the goodness, grace and glory of Christ, our Kinsman-Redeemer.

As we have seen in this book, *Ruth* represents all who are saved by the grace of God. *Boaz* represents the Lord Jesus Christ, our Kinsman-Redeemer. He is the owner of all things. All the fields of this world belong to him. He is the Master of all things. As Boaz was master in his house, so Christ is Master in his house, the church. Everything is subject to him. And he is the Master of the universe. His people obey him willingly, but all things obey him absolutely (John 17:2). The *field* in which Ruth gleaned represents the Word of God. The *young men*, the reapers, represent those who preach the gospel of Christ.

As Boaz commanded his young men to let fall some of the grain on purpose for Ruth, so the Lord Jesus Christ commands his servants, those who preach the gospel, to let fall precious truths on purpose for chosen sinners. In these two verses, we have instruction by example both for sinners who are seeking the Lord and preachers who are serving him.

**Seeking sinners**

Seeking sinners are like gleaners in a field. The old writers and preachers used to talk about 'sinners', 'sensible sinners', 'seeking sinners' and 'saved sinners'. I do not care much for those distinctions, as a general rule. Sinners are sinners. But the distinctions do serve a useful purpose.

A 'sinner' is a person under the wrath of God, lost and ruined in his sin, but utterly unaware of his sinful condition (Rom. 5:12).

A 'sensible sinner' is a sinner awakened to know his lost condition, a sinner under conviction, a sinner who knows that he is lost and needs Christ.

A 'seeking sinner' is one who knows he needs Christ and is seeking him. He feels his need of Christ, seeks him earnestly in his Word, in his house, by prayer and supplication, and will find him (Jer. 29:11-14). Like the four lepers of Elisha's day, he has resolved not to perish if life can be had (2 Kings 7:3-4). Like the Syro-Phoenician woman, such needy souls will not cease seeking the Lord God in Christ, and the mercy they need from him, until they have found him and obtained mercy (Mark 7:24-30).

A saved sinner is one who has come to Christ, one who trusts Christ as Lord and Saviour, one who believes on the Lord Jesus Christ.

When Ruth came into Boaz's field, she came as a gleaner seeking bread (2:2-3). As such, she is a picture of a sinner seeking the Lord in the house of bread.

### She was a Moabite

She belonged to a race that was under God's curse, and she knew it. She had no rights, except the rights of a stranger to glean in the fields. That is exactly our condition by nature. We belong to a race which is under the curse of God (Rom. 5:12; Eph. 2:1-4). We have no rights, but the right to pick up what God has left for sinners, the right to glean in his field.

### She had been reduced to a very low and poor condition (2:10)

She had once been very wealthy, married to Mahlon, daughter-in-law to Elimelech. Like her, all Adam's sons and daughters were once very wealthy. 'God made man upright' (Eccles. 7:29). Before the Fall, our father Adam possessed all God's creation and ruled over it. God gave man everything, even a righteous nature. But, like Ruth, fallen man is reduced to abject poverty (Eph. 2:11-12). Because she was poor, hungry, and in desperate need of help, she humbly took her place among the poor. Though she was a poor Moabitess, Ruth had resolved to seek and to follow the Lord God of Israel (1:16-17).

Blessed is that sinner who has been taught by the grace of God something of the abject poverty of his soul before God. Poor, hungry and in desperate need of help, he will humbly take his place in the dust before the throne of grace, seeking mercy (Heb. 4:16).

> I can but perish if I go,
> I am resolved to try;
> For if I stay away I know
> I must for ever die!
>
> Perhaps he will admit my plea,
> Perhaps will hear my prayer;
> But if I perish, I will pray
> And perish only there!

*Ruth had a very high opinion of Boaz's maidservants* (2:13)

She knew she was not like his maidservants, but she wanted to be. And those who seek Christ have a very high opinion of God's people. They know they are not like the children of God, but they want to be. They want forgiveness, righteousness and acceptance with God. They want to be found in Christ, accepted, at peace with God, possessing eternal life.

**Gospel preachers**

Gospel preachers may be compared to reapers. Christ himself will come as a reaper (Rev. 14:14-19), and he uses his servants as such. Preachers are reapers in two ways:

1. They reap the wheat and bind the tares of this world (Matt. 13:30; 2 Cor. 2:14-17). The preaching of the

gospel is God's ordained instrument both for salvation and condemnation.

2. They gather the wheat, the bread of God's Word, prepare it for his people, and feed them with knowledge and understanding (Jer. 3:15).

Every gospel preacher is responsible to feed the Lord's sheep. Those men who are called by God to do this great work are uniquely gifted and qualified by God for the work to which they are called (1 Tim. 3:1-7; Titus 1:5-9).

## Grain dropped on purpose

In keeping with the story before us, the preaching of the gospel is the scattering of handfuls of grain on purpose, the purposeful distribution of the bread gathered from the Word of God. Notice that Boaz gave his young men four strict commandments regarding Ruth. I take these to be four strict commandments from Christ to every man who preaches the gospel.

First, he says, 'Let her glean even among the sheaves.' Gospel preachers are not appointed by God to guard and protect the Word of God, giving it out in bits and pieces, as they see fit. Everything in the Book of God is profitable to his elect (2 Tim. 3:16-17). Let needy sinners glean anything they want, 'even among the sheaves'.

Secondly, Boaz said, 'Do not reproach her,' or 'Do not shame her.' How sad that any preacher should need to be told that, but many do. It is not the business of gospel preachers to chastise the Lord's children, but to comfort them (Isa. 40:1-2). As the man of God proclaims the gospel of God, when it is applied by the Spirit of God, it convicts, corrects, chastens and comforts the people of God.

Thirdly, Boaz said, 'Also let grain from the bundles fall purposely for her' (AV, 'Let fall also some of the handfuls of purpose for her'). I take that to mean that gospel preaching is to be plain and simple. Handfuls of grain are purposely left for specific people, with specific needs. They are left, not by the preacher's whims, but by the Spirit's direction. True preaching is personal, purposeful and passionate. God can make stones preach, but he uses men to preach to men. Only men feel what men feel. We are to scatter the Bread of Life with purpose, but by the handful — handfuls of promises, handfuls of doctrine, handfuls of grace!

Then Boaz repeated his first command using a stronger word: 'Do not rebuke her.' God's people do not belong to their pastors, teachers, elders, or visiting evangelists. They belong to God. It is not my place or yours to chastise his children. Yes, sometimes the faithful pastors and teachers must reprove and rebuke, but they must do it with all long-suffering and patience. Boaz's reapers understood that they were responsible to care for, protect and provide handfuls of grain on purpose for Ruth. They understood that she was distinctly the object of his love, and they treated her accordingly. 'So she gleaned'!

# 14.
# One who has the right to redeem

*'Then Naomi said to her daughter-in-law, "Blessed be he of the LORD, who has not forsaken his kindness to the living and the dead!" And Naomi said to her, "This man is a relation of ours, one of our close relatives"'* (Ruth 2:20).

Ruth 2:20; 4:1-10

The words 'one of our close relatives' might better be translated, 'one who has the right to redeem'. Boaz was the one who had the right to redeem Ruth, and Christ is the one who has the right to redeem his people.

It is impossible to understand what is written in Ruth chapters 3 and 4 unless we understand what is written in the law of God concerning redemption and the kinsman-redeemer. It will be profitable, therefore, to consider carefully the scriptures which deal with this subject.

Leviticus 25:25-28 gives us God's law regarding the redemption of property which had been sold:

> If one of your brethren becomes poor, and has sold some of his possession, and if his redeeming relative comes to redeem it, then he may redeem what his brother sold. Or if the man has no one to redeem it, but he himself becomes able to redeem it, then let him count the years since its sale, and restore the remainder to the man

to whom he sold it, that he may return to his possession. But if he is not able to have it restored to himself, then what was sold shall remain in the hand of him who bought it until the year of jubilee; and in the jubilee it shall be released, and he shall return to his possession.

Leviticus 25:47-48 records the law of God relating to the redemption of people who had sold themselves into bondage:

Now if a sojourner or stranger close to you becomes rich, and one of your brethren who dwells by him becomes poor, and sells himself to the stranger or sojourner close to you, or to a member of the stranger's family, after he is sold he may be redeemed again. One of his brothers may redeem him...

While we have no such specific laws in our modern culture, we do have similar ones with which we are familiar. An item that has been pawned, usually because of poverty, may be redeemed at the lawfully prescribed value by either the original owner or his lawful representative.

The word 'mortgage' is derived from two words meaning 'death' and 'pledge''. A mortgage is 'a death pledge'. That which is mortgaged becomes dead, or entirely lost, by the original owner's failure to pay.

As Jeremiah bought his cousin's field to set forth the certainty of God's promised deliverance (Jer. 32:6-12), so the Lord Jesus Christ has redeemed his elect. By the price of his infinitely meritorious blood, he has obtained eternal redemption for all his people (Heb. 9:12). His obtaining redemption for his people is the pledge of their certain deliverance from all sin and all its consequences by the grace of God.

Remember, the right of redemption was always dependent upon three things: first, kinship; secondly, ability; and, thirdly, willingness to redeem. The Son of God became our Kinsman by his incarnation. He is able to redeem, because he is himself both God and man. And he is a willing Redeemer (Heb. 12:1-2).

The word 'redeem' means 'to buy again', or 'buy back', and 'to take possession of'. The one who redeems evicts and dispossesses all those who have held his purchased property during the time of its bondage. He takes personal possession of that which has been bought back.

Redemption presupposes a dreadful calamity. It presupposes the sin and fall of all the human race in our father Adam (Rom. 5:12). Redemption by one who is near of kin also presupposes personal inability. The Israelite who was incapable of redeeming himself, who had to be redeemed by another, portrayed the fact that no sinner can redeem himself from the hands of divine justice (Ps. 49:6-9). Only the Son of God in human flesh could ransom us from the curse of the law. None but Christ could give infinitely meritorious satisfaction to the justice of God by the sacrifice of himself (Rom. 3:24-26).

That is what the Holy Spirit tells us Christ has done for every saved sinner. 'Christ has redeemed us' (Gal. 3:13). He bought us with his blood. Then, at the appointed time of love, he binds the strong man, casts him out of the house he has redeemed (the ransomed soul) and takes possession of the house himself. Soon, those possessed by his grace, to whom he has given the earnest of the Spirit, will be personally possessed by the Son of God (Eph. 1:7,14; Rom. 3:24-25; 8:23).

The Lord Jesus has redeemed all God's elect from the penalty of sin by his sin-atoning blood shed at Calvary (1 Peter 1:18-20). He redeems each one from the reigning power and dominion of sin by his Spirit's irresistible grace in regeneration (Rom. 6:17-18). And he will redeem them from the very being and all the evil consequences of sin in resurrection glory (Eph. 5:25-27).

In the book of Ruth, Boaz, her kinsman-redeemer, typifies and beautifully portrays the Lord Jesus Christ, our Kinsman-Redeemer. Here are seven characteristics of our Kinsman-Redeemer, seven characteristics of the one who has the right to redeem.

1. Redemption by a close relative is a matter of divine appointment. The kinsman-redeemer must be a divinely appointed redeemer. Only one who is appointed by God has the right to redeem (John 10:16-18; Heb. 10:5-14).

2. The one who has the right to redeem must be one who is near of kin to the person for whom he acts (Heb. 2:10-13).

3. The kinsman-redeemer must himself be entirely free of the debt (Heb. 7:26).

4. The one who has the right to redeem must be able to redeem. He must be able to satisfy fully all the demands of God's law and justice for those of his kin whom he represents.

5. The one who has the right to redeem must be willing to redeem. No one could be forced to redeem. The Lord Jesus Christ was Jehovah's willing bond-slave, because of his love for us (Exod. 21:5; Isa. 50:5-7).

6. The redemption made was always a particular and effectual redemption. There was nothing general, or universal about it. The redemption was made for specific people, and obtained a specific inheritance. The kinsman-redeemer restored what he had not taken away (Ps. 69:4). Our Lord Jesus Christ, by his glorious work of redemption, secured for a vast, innumerable multitude of sinners all the riches of eternal, heavenly glory (Rev. 7:9).

7. The one who has the right to redeem must raise up a seed. So also the Son of God, our Kinsman-Redeemer, will raise up a seed. There are some people in this world who, having been chosen by God in eternal election and redeemed by special redemption, must and shall be saved by God's omnipotent grace (Isa. 53:10-12; Ps. 22:30-31; Ruth 4:5-6).

# 15.
# Ruth comes to Boaz

*'And he said, "Who are you?" So she answered, "I am Ruth, your maidservant. Take your maidservant under your wing, for you are a close relative [margin, "redeemer"]'* (Ruth 3:9).

## Ruth 3:1-18

The Word of God is a declaration of redemption and grace in Christ. Not only does the Bible declare and explain God's great purpose and mighty operations of grace, it gives us numerous types, pictures and examples of it to which believers can relate. Here are some of them:

David and Mephibosheth (2 Sam. 9:1-13);
Ezekiel's deserted infant (Ezek. 16:1-8);
The valley of dry bones (Ezek. 37:1-14);
Hosea and Gomer (Hosea 1-3);
Lazarus' resurrection (John 11:1-46);
Zacchaeus' conversion (Luke 19:1-10);
The prodigal son (Luke 15:11-24);
The Good Samaritan (Luke 10:25-37);
Onesimus' conversion (Philem. 8-21).

Certainly, one of the most detailed and most beautifully instructive pictures of redemption and grace is the love story of Boaz and Ruth. Everyone likes a love story with a happy ending. The story begins with the declaration revealed in Elimelech's name: 'My God is King!' This story has two great themes, one hidden, the other revealed. The hidden theme is divine providence. The revealed theme is redemption (the Kinsman-Redeemer). This story of redemption and grace is a story about a great fall. Naomi went out full and came back empty (1:19-21). Her circumstances give a sad, sad portrait of the sin and fall of all the human race in our father Adam (Rom. 5:12). Ruth and Naomi came to Bethlehem at the beginning of the barley harvest, which was (as we have seen) a picture of this present gospel age. Ruth gleaned in the field of Boaz, portraying the way sinners find bread for their souls in the Word of God, through the ministry of the Word in God's house, the church.

Boaz took special notice of Ruth, just as the Lord Jesus Christ took special notice of chosen sinners before the world began. As Boaz commanded his young men not to touch Ruth, so Christ has commanded all things not to touch his chosen. God's elect are under his special protection (Hosea. 2:18; Rom. 8:28). As Boaz provided grain to be left on purpose, specifically for Ruth, so the Lord Jesus rules and commands all things specifically for his chosen ones (John 17:2). Boaz was Ruth's close relative, the one who had the right to redeem. As such, he portrays our great, incarnate God and Saviour, the Lord Jesus Christ (Heb. 2:9-18).

Here is a delightful point in this story of love, grace and redemption which is often overlooked. Boaz knew what his intentions were towards Ruth, just as Christ knew his intentions of love towards his people from eternity. He knew what he could and would do for Ruth, just as the Son of God knew what he could and would do for his church before the world began (Eph. 1:3-7; 5:25-27; 2 Tim. 1:9). Naomi also knew what Boaz could do if he was willing. The only one in the dark was Ruth, but she had seen Boaz. He had secured her attention.

In this third chapter, we see Ruth coming to Boaz. Here we have a beautiful, instructive picture of the way sinners come to Christ to obtain mercy and grace. Yet the story is as much for the benefit of those who have long been wedded to Christ as it is for those who have just begun to seek him. All who follow Ruth's example will find everlasting blessedness for their souls in Christ. 'As you therefore have received Christ Jesus the Lord, so walk in him.'

### Naomi's wise counsel (3:1-4)

In verses 1-4, Naomi, Ruth's mother-in-law, typically represents the church of God. The motherly characteristics of God's church are set before us throughout the Scriptures. She is a mother to all who are born of God (Isa. 49). Like a good mother, Naomi gave wise and godly counsel to Ruth. It is important to see that her counsel was indeed both wise and godly counsel. It was exactly according to the Word of God. It was designed by God to be a picture of grace:

> Then Naomi her mother-in-law said to her, "My daughter, shall I not seek security [literally "rest", margin] for you, that it may be well with you? Now Boaz, whose young women you were with, is he not our relative? In fact, he is winnowing barley tonight at the threshing-floor. Therefore wash yourself and anoint yourself, put on your best garment and go down to the threshing-floor; but do not make yourself known to the man until he has finished eating and drinking. Then it shall be, when he lies down, that you shall notice the place where he lies; and you shall go in, uncover his feet, and lie down; and he will tell you what you should do."'

Naomi sought Ruth's welfare, just as God's church in this world seeks the welfare of chosen sinners (3:1). She knew their kinsman-redeemer and had great confidence in him (3:2,18). Naomi knew who Boaz was, where he was and what he was able to do. These are the things she told Ruth. That is good witnessing! A good witness simply tells from personal experience and the testimony of Holy Scripture who Christ is, where he is to be found and what he is able to do for needy sinners.

Next, Naomi told Ruth exactly what she must do (3:3-4). If Ruth wanted to be married to Boaz, the decision was altogether up to Boaz, but she must let him know that she was interested. She must use every means at her disposal to obtain his favour. She must seek him. Yet she must seek him as one unworthy of his notice, as one totally dependent upon him. Naomi told Ruth to wash herself, go down to the threshing-floor, take note of the place where Boaz lay down and lay herself at his feet. Those who seek the Lord must seek him earnestly, with all their hearts (Jer. 29:11-13). As Ruth washed herself, so we must come to Christ in repentance, separating ourselves to him. If we desire to find Christ, we must put ourselves in the place where he is to be found, in the house of God (the public assembly of his saints), under the preaching of the gospel (Matt. 18:20; 1 Cor. 1:21).

Taking note of the place where he lies down — that is, taking note of the promises of God in the gospel to believing sinners — let us come to Christ, putting God in remembrance of them, as he commands us to do (Isa. 43:25-26). Like Ruth, we must prostrate ourselves at the feet of our great Boaz, if we desire to obtain that mercy and grace which only he can give. This is the place of humility, worship, reverence, faith and hope, and this is the place of blessing (Luke 7:36-50; 10:38-42). Just wait there! 'Do not make yourself known to the man... He will tell you what you should do.'

## Ruth's childlike obedience (3:5-7).

And she said to her, 'All that you say to me I will do.'

So she went down to the threshing-floor and did according to all that her mother-in-law instructed her. And after Boaz had eaten and drunk, and his heart was cheerful, he went to lie down at the end of the heap of grain; and she came softly, uncovered his feet, and lay down.'

Remember, Ruth was a grown woman. She had already been married once. She was probably between twenty and thirty years old. Yet she responded to godly instruction like a little child: 'All that you say to me I will do.' She did not know Boaz or the law of God, but Naomi did; so she listened to Naomi. She wanted Boaz. So she came to Boaz, softly. She ventured everything on his goodness. Imagine what could have happened to her! She came to him in the darkest hour of the night, at midnight.

## Ruth's humble, but bold request (3:8-9)

Now it happened at midnight that the man was startled, and turned himself; and there, a woman was lying at his feet.

And he said, 'Who are you?'

So she answered, 'I am Ruth, your maidservant. Take your maidservant under your wing [margin, "Or 'Spread the corner of your garment over your maidservant'"], for you are a close relative [margin, "redeemer"].'

Ruth had before offered a request to Boaz: 'Let me find favour in your sight, my lord...' (2:13). Here she offers herself. She made a plain confession of herself, her need and her utter dependence upon him. She said, 'I am Ruth,' a stranger, without claim or merit before you. 'I am … your maidservant,' your servant, at your disposal.

Then Ruth made a humble request. She said, 'Spread the corner of your garment over your maidservant.' That is to say, 'Take me to be yours.' This was a private, personal matter, between Ruth and Boaz alone. Not even Naomi could be involved in this. Faith in Christ is an intimate, personal thing.

Having laid herself, her condition and her needs before Boaz, Ruth then made one claim upon him. She said, 'You are a close relative.' With that claim she was saying, 'You have the right and the power to redeem me.' With the claim came the plea of her soul: 'Will you redeem me?' This is the way sinners in need of mercy come to the Saviour, and all who come to him obtain the mercy they seek (Matt. 8:2-3).

**Boaz's gracious promise** (3:10-13)

> Then he said, 'Blessed are you of the LORD, my daughter! For you have shown more kindness at the end than at the beginning, in that you did not go after young men, whether poor or rich. And now, my daughter, do not fear. I will do for you all that you request, for all the people of my town know that you are a virtuous woman. Now it is true that I am a close relative; however, there is a relative closer than I. Stay this night, and in the morning it shall be that if he will perform the duty of a close relative for you — good; let him do it. But if he does not want to perform the duty for you, then I will perform the duty for you, as the LORD lives! Lie down until morning.'

There was no reluctance at all on Boaz's part to perform the part of a kinsman-redeemer. He commended the wisdom of Ruth's choice. He promised to do all that she wanted. And he declared her to be a virtuous woman. She was not such by nature. She was by nature exactly the same as her sister-in-law, Orpah, a Moabite. But grace had wrought a wonderful change in her. It always does (1 Cor. 6:9-11; 2 Cor. 5:17).

Boaz was a willing redeemer, but something was more important to him than Ruth. Boaz would not act the redeemer's part if he could not do so in a way that honoured God. Redemption must honour God's holy law and righteous character (Rom. 3:24-26). Grace is never exercised at the expense of righteousness, justice and truth (Prov. 16:6).

## Ruth's confidence in Boaz (3:14-18)

> So she lay at his feet until morning, and she arose before one could recognize another.
>
> Then he said, 'Do not let it be known that the woman came to the threshing-floor.' Also he said, 'Bring the shawl that is on you and hold it.' And when she held it, he measured six ephahs of barley, and laid it on her. Then she went into the city.
>
> When she came to her mother-in-law, she said, 'Is that you, my daughter?' Then she told her all that the man had done for her. And she said, 'These six ephahs of barley he gave me; for he said to me, "Do not go empty-handed to your mother-in-law."'
>
> Then she said, 'Sit still, my daughter, until you know how the matter will turn out; for the man will not rest until he has concluded the matter this day.'

Notice the two 'I will's in this chapter. Ruth said to Naomi, concerning Boaz, 'All that you say to me I will do' (3:5). She was willing to follow the instruction of one who knew what was best for her soul. Then Boaz said to Ruth, 'I will do for you all that you request' (3:11). What a blessing! The Son of God is willing to grant believing sinners everything we need as a matter of free grace, and always does.

There are also two 'rests' in the chapter, two blessed portrayals of true sabbath-keeping. There was a rest for Ruth (3:1). This is the rest of faith. Sinners coming to Christ cease from their own works and rest in him (Matt. 11:28-29). There is also a rest for Boaz (3:18). The Lord Jesus Christ, once he finished the work of redemption for us, entered into his rest; and his rest is glorious (Heb. 4:10; Isa. 11:10).

Ruth stayed at Boaz's feet all night. Boaz took great care to protect her. And he provided her with all she needed. She had his heart. She was given his name. She had his grain. And she had him! When Ruth returned home she told Naomi all about Boaz. And Naomi assured Ruth of Boaz's faithfulness (3:18; Phil. 1:6; 1 Thess. 5:24).

The Lord Jesus Christ is to his people all that Boaz was to Ruth. He has done for us all that was pictured in Boaz's works of redemption for Ruth. We have obtained in him spiritually all that Ruth obtained in Boaz. Let us therefore give ourselves to him, as Ruth gave herself to Boaz, and live altogether for the honour of him who is our Kinsman-Redeemer (Rom. 12:1-2; 1 Cor. 6:19-20; Titus 2:10).

# 16.
# Three closer relatives, but only one Redeemer

*'Now it is true that I am a close relative; however, there is a relative closer than I. Stay this night, and in the morning it shall be that if he will perform the duty of a close relative for you — good; let him do it. But if he does not want to perform the duty for you, then I will perform the duty for you, as the LORD lives!'* (Ruth 3:12-13).

## Ruth 3:12-13

Tragedies alone never convert sinners (Rev. 9:20-21; 16:9-11). The old proverb is true: 'Any refuge built in the storm will die in the calm.' Acts of providential judgement do not produce repentance. A good scare will make a man seek a refuge, but it will not change his heart. Though these things are used by God to convert his elect, it is only when they are accompanied by the grace of God and a saving revelation of Christ that they change the heart and produce repentance (Zech. 12:10). 'The goodness of God leads you to repentance' (Rom. 2:4).

However, God does use providential tragedies, judgements and dangers to bring sinners whom he has chosen to Christ (Ps. 107:1-43). As we have seen, this fact is beautifully and clearly illustrated in the case of Ruth. Ruth, the chosen object of mercy, a Moabitess, must be saved. Therefore, God sent famine to Bethlehem in the land of Judah. Elimelech went down to Moab. Naomi, Orpah and Ruth were all widowed. All this was done to bring Ruth, the chosen object of mercy, to the place appointed by God for her to obtain mercy.

In the saving of chosen sinners, God always makes use of the preaching of the gospel (Rom. 10:10-17; 1 Cor. 1:21; James 1:18; 1 Peter 1:23-25). This fact is beautifully illustrated in Ruth 1:6. Almighty God never finds himself in a tight situation. He never needs to change his mind, or alter his purpose. At the appointed time, by one means or another, God will send someone to his elect with the good news of his free grace in Christ.

However, there is one thing absolutely essential to the salvation of God's elect, one thing without which no sinner could ever be saved, one thing without which God himself could never have saved anyone, and that is redemption by blood. 'Without shedding of blood there is no remission' (Heb. 9:22). God could save with or without earthly tragedies. Had he chosen to do so, certainly God could save without the ministry of the Word, had that been his purpose. But God cannot save apart from blood redemption. The whole purpose of the book of Ruth is to teach us about redemption — more specifically, to teach us about Christ, our Kinsman-Redeemer.

Boaz had spotted Ruth in his fields. He took care of Ruth and provided for her. Ruth came to Boaz on the threshing-floor and asked him to take her for his wife. He wanted her and was determined to have her; but the law of God had to be honoured. Ruth had an even closer relative. Boaz knew this closer relative. He knew that if Ruth looked to that man for redemption she would never be redeemed at all. Yet he had to be dealt with, according to the law.

Boaz was ready, at any price, to perform the part of a kinsman-redeemer to Ruth, the stranger from Moab. By nature, being a Moabitess, she was an aversion to him. Still, he loved her. He wanted her. But there was one more closely related than he to Elimelech's fallen family. So it is with the sons and daughters of Adam. Though there are many nearer to us by nature, there is none who could or would redeem us, but the Lord Jesus Christ, our Kinsman-Redeemer.

## The angels of God

Some commentators suggest that the closer relative represents the angels of God. Without question the angels are nearer kin to us than the Son of God in the natural order of creation. They are creatures like us. Christ is not a creature, but the Creator. The angels are the 'sons of God' by creation (Job 1:6). Christ is the eternal Son, one with and co-eternal with the eternal Father. Like us, angels were created to be the servants of God. The Lord Jesus became the Father's servant willingly (Isa. 50:5-7).

But redemption is a work no angel could ever perform. They might be able to assume human nature. They are holy creatures. But they are only finite creatures. They could never suffer the wrath of God to the full satisfaction of justice. They could never bring in everlasting righteousness. Besides, the angels of God were created to be ministering spirits to God's elect (Heb. 1:14). So far from being able to redeem, they look to redeemed sinners to learn about redemption (Eph. 3:10-11). What folly it is for blind idolaters to talk about praying to the angels! They have no power or ability to redeem and save. This is the work of God alone. Therefore, our prayers go out to God alone.

## The old man

Some are of the opinion that this closer relative represents the old man Adam — that is, our fallen nature. Both Philip Mauro[1]

and Ferrell Griswold[2] gave this interpretation to the passage.
The law of God certainly made allowance for the man in bondage to redeem himself, if he were able to do so (Lev. 25:26).
But that is a mighty big 'if'! If you are going to save yourself,
if you hope to redeem yourself, you have only to do three
things:

> 1. Perfectly obey God's holy law (Gal. 3:10);
> 2. Make complete atonement for all your sin (Exod.
> 13:13);
> 3. Give yourself a new heart (see Isa. 1:16-18).

Saving oneself is an utter impossibility! As both Mauro and
Griswold pointed out, it is permissible, but it is not possible.
No mere man can obey God's law. No mortal can atone for sin
and satisfy the infinite justice of the holy Lord God. And no
man can make himself a new creature! Only the infinite God
himself can do these things.

Not only is saving oneself impossible; it is also impossible
for any man to redeem another man (Ps. 49:7-9). We are but
finite creatures of the dust. Redemption requires an infinite
Saviour, with infinite righteousness, infinitely meritorious blood
and infinite power. That is just the kind of Redeemer the Lord
Jesus Christ is (Heb. 10:5-14).


**The law of God**

A third closer relative to us is the law of God. The law of God
is holy, just and good. It was made for man, for the benefit of
man. The law, in its entirety, with all its rigours, commands,
earthly ordinances, sacrifices and legal ceremonies, was designed by God to bring us to and to shut us up to Christ as our
only Saviour (Gal. 3:24). But the law of God could never

redeem and save fallen man (Rom. 8:3; Gal. 3:21; 4:5-6; Heb. 10:1-4).

The law curses, but never cures. The law provides punishment, but not propitiation. The law bruises, but never blesses. The law gives terror, but never peace. As John Berridge wrote:

> The law demands a weighty debt,
> And not a single mite will bate;
> The gospel sings of Jesus' blood,
> And says it made the payment good.
>
> The law provokes men oft to ill,
> And churlish hearts makes harder still;
> The gospel acts the kinder part
> And melts the hard and stubborn heart.
>
> 'Run, run, and work,' the law commands,
> Yet finds me neither feet nor hands;
> But sweeter news the gospel brings;
> It bids me fly, and gives me wings!
>
> (Such needful wings, O Lord, impart,
> To brace my feet and brace my heart;
> Good wings of faith and wings of love
> Will make the cripple sprightly move.)
>
> With these my lumpish soul may fly,
> And soar aloft, and reach the sky;
> Nor faint, nor falter in the race,
> But cheerfully work and sing of grace.

As Ruth's closer relative was unable and thus unwilling to redeem her, so these three closer relatives of ours are incapable of redeeming our souls. But, blessed be God, there is one who has made himself nearer of kin to us than any others, and he is both able and willing to redeem!

## Christ alone

The Lord Jesus Christ is our one and only Kinsman-Redeemer. The Son of God has made himself our Kinsman that he might be our Redeemer (2 Cor. 8:9; Heb. 2:10-18). He took our human nature into union with his divine nature, so that he might redeem us from the curse of the law by the sacrifice of himself. Someone once said, 'God could not suffer and man could not satisfy; but the God-man has both suffered and satisfied.' The Lord Jesus Christ, our Kinsman-Redeemer, has willingly fulfilled the part of the redeeming relative for us. Christ is a willing Saviour. He willingly became Jehovah's servant, because he loved us (Exod. 21:1-6).

He is an able Saviour, too (Heb. 7:25). He has done everything for us that the law of God required a relative to do. He paid our debt. He redeemed us from bondage. He married the desolate. He raised up children to the dead, a seed to serve him for ever. The love of Christ for us far exceeds the love of any on this earth: 'We love him because he first loved us' (1 John 4:19). As his love for us exceeds all earthly loves, let our love for him exceed all earthly loves as well.

# 17.
# Boaz redeems Ruth

*'And Boaz said to the elders and to all the people, "You are witnesses this day that I have bought all that was Elimelech's... Moreover, Ruth the Moabitess, the widow of Mahlon, I have acquired as my wife, to perpetuate the name of the dead through his inheritance"'* (Ruth 4:10).

## Ruth 4:1-22

We come now to the climax of the book of Ruth. The events recorded in chapter 4 are the things to which everything up to this point has been leading. Everything in this chapter is designed by God the Holy Spirit to direct our hearts and minds to the Lord Jesus Christ and his great work of redemption.

'Now Boaz went up to the gate and sat down there' (4:1). Why? To intercede for Ruth. This is a picture of our Lord Jesus Christ who has gone up to heaven for us, and sat down there to intercede for us. Boaz went up to the city to do his work; Christ has gone up to heaven because his work is done (Heb. 10:11-14; 1:1-3). Just as everything Boaz did as he sat at the gate of the city was for Ruth, so everything Christ does is for his people. Failure was not even considered. Boaz was resolved to take Ruth home with him as his bride. With our great Saviour, failure is an impossibility (Isa. 42:4). 'He will save his people from their sins' (Matt. 1:21).

Boaz said to his relative, 'If you will redeem it, redeem it; but if you will not redeem it, then tell me, that I may know; for there is no one but you to redeem it, and I am next after you' (4:4). This close relative, more than anything else, represents the law. But the law cannot redeem; it cannot save without incurring damage to itself and the very character of God. The law identifies sin, but cannot forgive it. The law condemns us all, but changes none. The law slays, but can never save (Rom. 3:19-20,28; 8:3-4; Gal. 3:10,13).

Next Boaz said, 'On the day you buy the field from the hand of Naomi, you must also buy it from Ruth the Moabitess.' Ruth, representing the sinner saved by the grace of God in Christ, is also typical of the church of God's elect. The world is a great field. The church of God is a treasure hid in the field (Matt. 13:44). Our heavenly Boaz, the Lord Jesus Christ, sold all that he had and bought the field so that he might get the treasure.

As a man, as the God-man Mediator, our Lord Jesus Christ purchased all things. All things are his. He rules and disposes of all things for the saving of his people, whom he redeemed with his own blood. As Boaz bought all that was Elimelech's, so Christ bought all that was Adam's. As God the Son, it was his before. But now it is his by right of redemption as our mediator (Ps. 2:8; John 17:2; Rom. 14:9).

'And Boaz said to the elders and all the people, "You are witnesses this day that I have bought all that was Elimelech's... Moreover, Ruth the Moabitess ... I have acquired as my wife"' (4:9-10). Boaz bought all that was Elimelech's, but the object of his love and the purpose of his work was Ruth. As Boaz purchased Ruth to be his wife, so the Lord Jesus Christ purchased the church of God's elect to be his wife (Eph. 5:25-27). The object of his love, the purpose of his work was the salvation of his people. Here are nine things about Boaz's redemption of Ruth which are also true concerning Christ's redemption of God's elect.

## 1. A proper redemption

None but Boaz could redeem Ruth. He alone was both able and willing to redeem. Redemption, if it is proper, must be legal. And our redemption by Christ is a proper redemption. Deliverance without satisfaction is a violation of the law, and satisfaction without deliverance is a violation of justice. Christ alone is able to redeem us (Ps. 24:3-6). He alone is willing to redeem us at the price demanded by divine justice (Heb. 10:1-5). Christ alone is a just and legal Redeemer for sinners (Isa. 45:21).

## 2. A pleasurable redemption

Boaz went to great pains and incurred considerable trouble and cost to himself in order to redeem Ruth, but he did so with great pleasure. He did it all with the sweet prospect of having Ruth for himself. In the same way, our Lord Jesus found great pleasure and satisfaction in the midst of his sorrows, as he anticipated having his elect with him for ever (Heb. 12:2; Isa. 53:10-12).

Our dear Saviour did not hesitate to pay the price required for our ransom. He willingly took our sins upon himself. He willingly took for us the cup of wrath. He willingly gave himself for us, that he might redeem us from the curse of the law.

> Here's the compassion of our God —
> That when Christ, our Saviour, knew
> The price of pardon was his blood,
> His pity ne'er withdrew!

### 3. A precious redemption

Naomi, Ruth and all who understood what he did esteemed
Boaz's condescending work of redeeming her a matter of great
grace, a precious deed on the part of one who made himself
precious in their eyes (Ruth 2:20; 4:11-14). So also, all who
have tasted the free grace of God in Christ count him, his
blood and his redemption precious (2 Cor. 9:15; 1 Peter 1:18-20;
2:7). The redemption of our souls is precious (Ps. 49:8) because the price of our ransom was Christ's precious blood.

Our redemption by Christ is also a precious thing because
it was a great act of infinitely great and condescending grace.
Boaz was not ashamed of Ruth, the poor Moabite stranger.
She could not redeem herself, but this wealthy nobleman
stooped to lift her up and exalt her. What a great type of the
Lord Jesus Boaz is! The Son of God stooped low (2 Cor. 8:9;
Phil. 2:5-8) that he might lift us high. The great Prince of
Heaven calls to himself the poor, the wretched, the miserable,
the halt, the lame and the blind. And he is never ashamed to
identify himself with them and to own them as his own brethren (Heb. 2:9-11). As the great Boaz redeemed and married
the lowly Ruth; as the great King David took the poor, crip-
pled son of Jonathan, Mephibosheth, into his house and caused
him to sit at his table as one of the king's own sons; as Hosea
redeemed the wretched Gomer and took her to be his wife
after she had defiled herself so horribly — so the Lord Jesus
Christ has redeemed and married us (1 Cor. 1:26-29).

### 4. A public redemption (4:1-2)

> Now Boaz went up to the gate and sat down there; and
> behold, the close relative of whom Boaz had spoken
> came by. So Boaz said, 'Come aside, friend, sit down
> here.' So he came aside and sat down.

And he took ten men of the elders of the city, and said, 'Sit down here.' So they sat down (4:1-2).

There were many witnesses to this great transaction. This thing was not done in a corner. When Boaz purchased Ruth everyone in Bethlehem knew it. So, too, there were many witnesses to the redemption of God's elect by Christ. As the angels of God observed the great work when God the Father forsook his darling Son, who was made to be sin for us, the sun was darkened, the earth quaked, the stones split open, the graves were opened and the veil in the temple was ripped apart from the top to the bottom. The law of God being satisfied, the veil was ripped apart, showing that there is now open access for sinners to come to the holy Lord God by the blood of Christ. As Satan and the demons of hell observed the dying triumph of the God-man, all hell must have trembled!

Then, three days later, our great emancipator rose from the grave! As Boaz pulled off his shoe as a token of the transaction being complete (4:8), so the Lord Jesus Christ took off his grave-clothes and ascended up to heaven, 'having obtained eternal redemption' for us (Heb. 9:12; Rom. 4:25).

## 5. A purposeful redemption (4:10)

Moreover, Ruth the Moabitess, the widow of Mahlon, I have acquired as my wife, to perpetuate the name of the dead through his inheritance, that the name of the dead may not be cut off from among his brethren and from his position at the gate. You are witnesses this day (4:10).

Boaz redeemed Ruth 'that the name of the dead may not be cut off'. And the Lord Jesus redeemed unto himself a people to be his seed, his own special people, to live for ever (Ps. 22:30; Isa. 53:10; Titus 2:14). Boaz redeemed Ruth to be his wife — not his slave, but his wife. So, too, the Son of God redeemed us to be part of his bride, the church. What a great boon of grace it would have been for such as we are to have been purchased as his slaves! But here is God's super-abounding grace to sinners — Christ has purchased a people unfit to be his slaves to be his holy bride for ever!

## 6. A particular redemption (4:10)

'Ruth, the Moabitess, the widow of Mahlon, I have acquired...' (4:10). Let unbelieving religious men argue and debate as they will, the blood of Christ was shed for and redeemed a particular people. There is not even a hint of universal redemption to be found in Holy Scripture. Everywhere in the Bible, when redemption is typified, prophesied and explained, it is set forth as being the particular, effectual redemption of a specifically chosen people called 'the elect' (Isa. 53:8; Acts 20:28; Gal. 3:13; Eph. 5:25-27; Titus 2:14; Rev. 5:9).

## 7. A productive redemption

Boaz acquired Ruth as his wife. That was his purpose, and it was accomplished. Be assured, the Lord Jesus Christ will also accomplish his purpose. He will obtain his Moabite bride. As a direct result of this great transaction God brought his king to his holy hill of Zion (4:17,22). So, too, the Lord Jesus Christ, David's great son and his Lord, was brought into his kingdom and made to sit upon his throne by means of the redemption he accomplished at Calvary (Acts 2:22-36). As a result of this redemption of Ruth, the Son of God was brought into this world (Matt. 1:5). And as the result of that redemption ac-complished in the death of Christ all God's elect will be brought into heavenly glory (Gal. 3:13-14). A redemption which accomplishes nothing is a useless redemption. Such redemption is not found in the Bible.

## 8. A perfect redemption

'Boaz took Ruth and she became his wife' (4:13). So too, our heavenly Boaz will conclude this matter when the day is over. He will come again to take his Bride unto himself (Rev. 19:1-9). What a day that will be!

## 9. A praiseworthy redemption

There is no praise in this whole affair for Ruth, the one who is redeemed. All praise goes to Boaz, the redeemer. The work of redemption was all his. Therefore, he was praised for it (4:11). Boaz was made famous in Israel. His house was filled. Why? Because he deserved it. So also, our great God and Saviour, the Lord Jesus Christ, has been made great. He alone is famous in God's Israel. His house shall be filled. Why? Because he deserves it!

Let us adore and publish the name of our dear Redeemer. Make him famous where you live for his sovereign purpose of grace, for his electing love, for his adorable providence, for his immaculate mercy and for his great, effectual redemption of our souls by his precious blood. Do not allow the cares of this world to destroy you, as they did Elimelech. Cling to Christ, as Ruth did to Naomi. Cast yourself upon his mercy continually, as she cast herself upon the goodness and mercy of Boaz.

# 18.
# 'To raise up the name of the dead'

*'Then Boaz said, "On the day you buy the field from the hand of Naomi, you must also buy it from Ruth the Moabitess, the wife of the dead, to perpetuate [literally, 'raise up'] the name of the dead through his inheritance"'* (Ruth 4:5).

## Ruth 4:4-8

In the fourth chapter of Ruth, we are told how Boaz cleared away all obstacles to his redemption of, and union with, Ruth. Remember, the purpose of his heart was settled. He had made up his mind to redeem Ruth and to marry her. But he was an honourable man. He would not redeem her, he would not marry her, he would not have her as his wife unless he could do so in a way that would completely honour God and his holy law. So the claims of the closer relative had to be dealt with before Boaz could take Ruth for himself. Therefore, he came to the gate of the city, called together the elders of the city and spoke publicly to the man who was Ruth's closer relative by virtue of her marriage to Mahlon. The conversation is recorded for us in Ruth 4:4-8.

Clearly, the prominent subject of this passage is redemption. The word 'redeem' is used nine times in these five verses. The purpose, or object, of redemption is plainly stated in verse 5. It is 'to perpetuate [literally, "raise up"] the name of the dead'. The object of redemption, both typical and real, is to raise up the seed of a man who has died, for the honour of that man.

According to the law of God (the law which was given to portray and point us to the Lord Jesus Christ), the duty of the close relative, the kinsman-redeemer, involved three things. He was obligated by the law of God to do these things. If he failed to do them he must bear public reproach for his failure (Deut. 25:5-10; Lev. 25:25-26). The kinsman-redeemer must:

1. Restore the inheritance of his impoverished relative;
2. Procure the liberty of his brother who through poverty had been brought into slavery;
3. Marry his dead relative's wife and 'raise up' the name of the dead'.

As Boaz did these things for Ruth, so our Lord Jesus Christ, the Son of God, has done all this for God's elect. He has redeemed the inheritance we lost in Adam. He restored what he did not take away. He procured our liberty. By his blood he freed us from the curse of the law. And by the power of his grace he has broken the iron fetters that held us in slavery to Satan and to sin. By the power of his grace, by his omnipotent Spirit, our Kinsman-Redeemer, the Lord Jesus Christ, is raising up the name of the dead in this world.

## A matter of public record

Redemption was always a matter of indisputable, public record. God arranged his law in such a way that throughout the history of Israel in the Old Testament, every transaction involving redemption was done in public, attested to by numerous witnesses and recorded as a matter of public record, so that the transaction could never be nullified or disputed. As we read this fourth chapter of Ruth, several things stand out as matters of obvious significance.

First, the matter dealt with here is *a matter of great importance*. Boaz came to the gate of the city, called the elders together, and a large crowd immediately assembled. They knew that something of great importance was about to take place. Something more was involved in this business than Ruth and Mahlon, Naomi and her daughter-in-law. That which was about to take place, that which was being discussed, had something to do with the glory of God, the purpose of God and the people of God. Redemption is a subject of immense importance. This is more than a doctrinal statement. It is the revelation of God's glory (Rom. 3:24-26), the declaration of his purpose (Rom. 8:28) and the hope of his people (2 Cor. 5:21).

Second, this business was transacted in *a conspicuous, public place*: 'Now Boaz went up to the gate and sat down there.' Not only is the work of Christ in redemption a matter of vital importance; it has been accomplished in a public manner (Acts 26:26-27; 2:22-23). The law and the prophets all pointed to this as the climatic event for which God created all things. The apostles all speak of Christ's work of redemption as the crucial issue of the gospel. As we saw in the previous chapter, the darkened sun, the earthquake, the opened graves and the rent veil all attested to the fact that the man who died at Calvary was, as the centurion said, 'the Son of God'.

Third, redemption was *a legal matter*. It was a legal transaction. It was done according to the law, and it honoured the law. There is an impressive scene before us (4:2). Boaz took ten men of the city, ten elders in Israel, to be witnesses to what took place. I cannot help thinking that these ten men are suggestive of God's holy law, summarized in the Ten Commandments. Our Lord Jesus fulfilled both the law and the prophets when he died as our substitute and redeemed us. He fulfilled the righteousness required by the law's commandments in his life (Jer. 23:5-6). He fulfilled the penalty required by the law's justice (Gal. 3:13). He fulfilled the prophets, suffering to the last detail 'all that was written concerning him' (Acts 13:29; John 19:28; Luke 24:44-46). Thus, it is written: 'Christ is the end of the law for righteousness to everyone who believes' (Rom. 10:4).

## The impotence of the law

The failure of the closer relative to redeem Ruth demonstrates the inability of the law to save man. We are not told what the man's motives were. Whatever they may have been, the closer relative preferred to suffer public shame and disgrace rather than redeem Ruth and thus ruin his own inheritance. As we have seen, this closer relative, more than anything else, stands out in the book of Ruth as a picture of God's holy law.

The law of God is holy, just and good, but it cannot forgive sin or extend mercy without marring its justice. The law always identifies and exposes sin. It condemns the sinner, without regard to, or giving any consideration to, age, environment, education, gender, parentage, or extenuating circumstances: 'The soul who sins shall die'! The law takes only one thing into consideration — justice, strict, absolute, unbending justice. It identifies sin, exposes sin and condemns sin. It has no other purpose and no other ability (Rom. 3:19-20; 7:9; 8:3).

All who attempt salvation by the law, all who attempt to come to God on their own merits, will, like this closer relative, bear the reproach publicly for ever. What the closer relative could not and would not do for Ruth, Boaz gladly did. And what the law could not and would not do for us, the Lord

Jesus Christ gladly did. As Boaz was delighted to redeem Ruth, Christ was delighted to redeem his people, because of his great love for us (Rom. 8:1-4).

The closer relative pulled off his shoe — a sign of disgrace, slavery and disavowed ownership (Deut. 25:9) — and Boaz stepped into his shoes. Moses (the representative of the law) put off his shoes as a servant before God's manifest presence. Believers, as the sons of God, have had the shoes of liberty and sonship put on their feet in the Father's house (Luke 15:22). The legalist (the person who attempts to gain God's favour by his own works) is a slave, cursed by the very thing that makes him so proud (Gal. 3:10). We are the sons of God, accepted in the Beloved (Eph. 1:6; 1 John 3:1).

### 'To raise up the name of the dead'

As Boaz assumed and discharged every duty of a kinsman-redeemer for Ruth, so the Lord Jesus Christ assumed and fully discharged the whole work of redemption for us. Not only did Boaz buy the inheritance that Mahlon had lost, he bought it for Ruth particularly. He bought the field and redeemed Ruth for this purpose — 'to raise up the name of the dead'. Soon Obed was born to Ruth and Boaz.

In the same way our Lord Jesus Christ redeemed us to raise up the name of the dead, to raise up a seed from among the fallen sons and daughters of Adam to serve him — and it shall be done! 'A seed shall serve him.' 'He shall not fail!'

As Judah assumed all responsibility for Benjamin as his voluntary surety, so the Lord Jesus Christ assumed all responsibility for God's elect in the covenant of grace before the world began (Gen. 43:9; Heb. 7:22). The Son of God came into this world, lived, died and rose again to save his people from their sins (Matt. 1:21). God the Father has given his Son, our Saviour, the power to give eternal life to all his chosen seed (John 17:2). Therefore, we are assured that all who were given to Christ in the covenant of grace before the world began, all who were redeemed by his blood, all for whom he came into this world, he will present faultless before the presence of the divine glory at last (John 6:37-40; 10:16; 1 Cor. 15:28; Heb. 2:13). The immutability of God's love demands it (Mal. 3:6). The steadfastness of God's purpose demands it (Titus 1:2). The justice of God's character demands it. Augustus Toplady said it well:

Payment God cannot twice demand,
First at my bleeding Surety's hand,
And then again at mine!

The intercession of Christ demands the salvation of those for whom he lived, died and rose again (John 17:24). Indeed, the honour of our Boaz, the honour of Christ, demands it. If he should fail to save those whom he came to save, if he should fail fully, effectually and everlastingly to redeem even one whom he came to redeem, he must bear the shame for ever; and that cannot be. Our Kinsman-Redeemer shall, at last, see the results of the labour of his soul with complete satisfaction.

# 19.
# Seven lessons from the book of Ruth

*'Blessed be the L*ORD*, who has not left you this day without a redeemer; and may his name be famous in Israel!'* (Ruth 4:14, marginal reading).

Ruth 1:1 - 4:22

The story of Ruth and her kinsman-redeemer has special appeal to believers, because we see in Ruth and Boaz an outline of our own spiritual history and of our relationship with the Lord Jesus Christ, our Kinsman-Redeemer, of whom Boaz was merely a type. I have not attempted to give a thorough exposition of this blessed little history. I leave that to others who are more capable. It has been my purpose simply to show forth the grace and glory of God in Christ, our Kinsman-Redeemer, as he is portrayed in these four chapters. In this final chapter, we shall take an overview of the entire book. We will begin at Ruth 1:1, and pick up seven of the golden nuggets scattered through these four chapters.

In these four chapters, the Holy Spirit clearly sets before us seven specific lessons regarding the grace of God, redemption by Christ and our relationship to him by faith.

## 1. The cost of unbelief and disobedience

The first lesson is a very sad and regrettable one, but one we all must learn. It is set before us in the very first verse of the first chapter. Here we are taught the cost of unbelief and disobedience: 'Now it came to pass, in the days when the judges ruled, that there was a famine in the land. And a certain man of Bethlehem, Judah, went to dwell in the country of Moab, he and his wife and his two sons.'

In a time of famine, Elimelech, whose name means, 'My God is King', took what he determined was a prudent step. He moved to Moab. But his move was a very costly one. The move was instigated and made by selfishness and unbelief, and ended in tragedy. Elimelech died in Moab and left his family in a godless, pagan land, far away from the people of God, the house of God and the Word of God. Elimelech's disobedience led his sons into disobedience. They both married Moabite women. Elimelech's move to Moab cost him dearly. There he died in poverty. Both his sons died in poverty and disobedience to God. His wife was reduced to a bitter existence (1:20-21). Elimelech reminds me a great deal of Lot. Let all who are wise learn from Elimelech's error:

> It is always less costly to obey God.
> All disobedience is manifest unbelief.
> Bad decisions made early in life will have bad consequences in years to come.
> Our example is at least as important as our words, and probably much more important.
> Do not, for any reason, move your family anywhere you would not want to die and leave them.

## 2. God's sovereign, unconditional election

The second thing clearly taught in this book is God's sovereign, unconditional election: 'Then she arose with her daughters-in-law that she might return from the country of Moab, for she had heard in the country of Moab that the LORD had visited his people in giving them bread' (1:6). Ruth was a Moabitess, the daughter of a cursed race. She was a stranger. Some suggest that her name means 'Satisfied Stranger'. Ruth was a stranger to God by nature, but she found satisfaction in the Lord God by grace. Ruth was chosen by God to be an heir of eternal salvation in Christ. Let us ever rejoice in, and give thanks to, our God for his free, electing love in Christ (Ps. 65:4; John 15:16; Eph. 1:3-6; 2 Thess. 2:13; 1 Thess. 5:9). God's election is an eternal, unconditional, immutable act of love and grace to sinners in Christ, by which all the blessings of grace are secured to the objects of his love.

## 3. The mystery of God's providence

Thirdly, the book of Ruth beautifully unfolds the wondrous mystery of God's wise and adorable providence. Providence is the unfolding and accomplishment of God's everlasting purpose, which is the salvation of his elect (Rom. 8:28-30). Once we reach the end of the story, especially reading it with hindsight and in the light of the completed volume of inspired Holy Scripture, we can see God's providence in everything that took place in this story.

Providence brought the famine in Bethlehem and gave bounty in Moab. Elimelech's move was an act of great wickedness on his part, for which he alone was entirely responsible, but even that was totally ruled by God's sovereign providence and according to his eternal purpose of grace (Ps. 76:10). Let no one imagine that the family bloodline of our Saviour was left to chance! The Lord God had chosen Ruth as an heir of his grace and to be the ancestral grandmother of our Lord's earthly family (Matt. 1:5). Therefore, Elimelech came to Moab. Then, at God's appointed time, Naomi heard good news in Moab, good news of God visiting his people in mercy (Ruth 1:6). By the arrangement of special providence, Ruth came to the field of Boaz (2:3). There, Boaz (the type of our sovereign Lord and Redeemer) commanded his young men to protect her, drop handfuls of grain on purpose for her and let her drink from his fountains. Will we ever learn to trust God's providence?

> God moves in a mysterious way
> His wonders to perform;
> He plants his footsteps in the sea
> And rides upon the storm.
>
> Deep in unfathomable mines
> Of never-failing skill
> He treasures up his bright designs
> And works his sovereign will!

## 4. The blessedness of redemption by Christ

Fourthly, this little book is most precious, because it sets before us in a beautiful, typical picture the blessedness of redemption by Christ: 'Then Naomi said to her daughter-in-law, "Blessed be he of the LORD, who has not forsaken his kindness to the living and the dead!" And Naomi said to her, "The man is a relation of ours, one of our redeemers' (2:20, marginal reading). What a beautiful picture of Christ Boaz is!

1. He was a kinsman-redeemer. Christ assumed our nature: 'The Word became flesh.'

2. He was a mighty redeemer. Our blessed Saviour is mighty indeed. His name is 'the Mighty God'!

3. Boaz was a wealthy redeemer. Christ is filled with infinite, inexhaustible treasures of grace for sinners.

4. He was a willing redeemer. Christ willingly laid down his life for us.

5. He was a lawful redeemer, such a redeemer as the law required. So, too, is our Lord Jesus Christ.

5. Boaz was an effectual redeemer. He purchased Ruth, the object of his love, for his own. The Son of God, our effectual Redeemer, will have as his own the people of his choice.

6. Boaz was a complete redeemer, too. When Ruth married Boaz, she received him and everything in him. And it is written, concerning all God's elect, 'You are complete in him' (Col. 2:10).

## 5. The instrumentality of God's Word in conversion

I am not straining inspiration at all when I say that the fifth lesson set before us in the book of Ruth is the instrumentality of the Word in conversion: 'Then she arose with her daughters-in-law that she might return from the country of Moab, for she had heard in the country of Moab that the LORD had visited his people by giving them bread' (1:6). God has ordained the salvation of his people and he has ordained the means by which he will save them. When the appointed time of love comes, when God is pleased to call the sinner he has chosen to life and faith in Christ, he will do so by sending someone to the chosen sinner with the gospel of his grace. To many, this teaching seems inconsistent with the message of God's sovereign grace, but man's inability to comprehend the consistency of Scripture does not alter the plain statements of

Holy Scripture. And the Scriptures plainly declare that God saves sinners only by the instrumentality of the gospel: 'It pleased God through the foolishness of the message preached to save those who believe' (1 Cor. 1:21; Rom. 10:17; Eph. 1:13; Heb. 4:12; James 1:18; 1 Peter 1:23-25).

## 6. The character of true faith

Next, the book of Ruth shows us the character of true faith. True faith is commitment to Christ.

But Ruth said:

> 'Entreat me not to leave you,
> Or to turn back from following after you;
> For wherever you go, I will go;
> And wherever you lodge, I will lodge;
> Your people shall be my people,
> And your God, my God.
> Where you die, I will die,
> And there will I be buried.
> The LORD do so to me, and more also,
> If anything but death parts you and me.'
>
> When she saw that she was determined to go with her, she stopped speaking to her
>
> (1:16-18).

The difference between Ruth and Orpah was commitment. True faith acknowledges personal unworthiness (2:10) and humbly takes its place at the feet of Christ (3:4-8). This is the place where Mary was found, hearing the Saviour's words. The leper fell at the Master's feet when he came seeking mercy.

When John saw Christ in his glory and heard his voice, he fell at his feet. Let us ever be found 'at his feet'. This is the place of humility, reverence, faith, worship, rest, love and honour. We serve Christ best when we serve at his feet, leaning upon his Word, trusting his grace, seeking his glory.

## 7. The reward of faith

Finally, this precious little book gives a hint regarding the reward of faith: 'The LORD repay your work, and a full reward be given you by the LORD God of Israel, under whose wings you have come for refuge' (2:12). Faith is taking shelter under the wings of the Almighty, fleeing to Christ our refuge. Faith, above all else, honours God. And faith obtains the reward of grace. Our faith in Christ is not the cause of God's grace to us. Indeed, our faith in him is the gift and operation of his grace (Eph. 1:19; 2:8-9; Col. 2:12). Yet, it is by faith that we obtain the enjoyment and blessedness of all the blessings of God's grace in Christ. When we believe on the Lord Jesus Christ, all that he is becomes ours. All grace is ours. All things in time are ours. All things in eternity are ours. If Christ is ours, all is ours!

The Lord Jesus Christ is our great Boaz. In him we are blessed with all spiritual blessings, from everlasting to everlasting. 'Blessed be the LORD, who has not left you this day without a redeemer; and may his name be famous in Israel.' Amen.

# Notes

**Chapter 4 — Good news heard in Moab**
1. Mauro, Phillip, *Ruth, The Satisfied Stranger,* Fleming H. Revel, Old Tappan, New Jersey, 1920, pp.63-4.

**Chapter 6 — 'The beginning of barley harvest'**
1. Mauro, *Ruth The Satisfied Stranger,* p.88.

**Chapter 16 — Three closer relatives, but only one Redeemer**
1. Mauro, *Ruth The Satisfied Stranger,* p.205.
2. Ferrell Griswold, *Ruth* (series of sermons delivered to the First Baptist Church of Minor Heights, Birmingham, Alabama).

The Lord Jesus is everywhere to be found in Scripture. As Luke records how he made his journey with some of his disciples along the road to Emmaus, he emphasizes how he explained how the Scriptures pointed to him.

Not long after that event, the apostles and leaders of the early church went about preaching Christ from the Scriptures – naturally what we, today, call the Old Testament.

To help you see Christ in all the Scriptures, we publish a number of books with this great theme running centrally through them.

*Discovering Christ in Ruth: The Kinsman-Redeemer*
Don Fortner
085234435X, 144 pages

This is a book which will give you many insights into what Scripture suggests about Christ typified through the experiences of Ruth and Boaz.

*A Son is Promised: Christ in the Psalms*
Harry Uprichard
0852343272, 144 pages

Here is a look at select psalms which are quoted in the New Testament and which apply to Christ.

*He is altogether lovely: Discovering Christ in the Song of Solomon*
Roger Ellsworth
0852344066, 240 pages

This is a book written in the author's usual engaging style that leads you in a warm and fresh way to Christ and the great teachings of the Christian faith.


*A Son is given: Christ in Isaiah*
Harry Uprichard
0852343019, 160 pages

Read about the Lord Jesus in all his glory – his coming, his kingdom, his salvation, his works, his death and the great gospel of his grace.


*A Son is Revealed: Discovering Christ in the book of Mark*
Harry Uprichard
085234418X, 160 pages

This book has been written to help you keep pace with John Mark's fast-moving account of the last years of Christ's ministry.

A wide range of excellent books on spiritual subjects is available from Evangelical Press. Please write to us for your free catalogue or contact us by e-mail.

Evangelical Press
Grange Close, Faverdale North Industrial Estate, Darlington, Co. Durham, DL3 0PH, England

Evangelical Press USA
P. O. Box 84, Auburn, MA 01501, USA

e-mail: sales@evangelical-press.org

web: www.evangelical-press.org